MY AMERICA STORY BOOK

Mexican / Civil Wars

A Compilation of Historical
Biographies for the Young Reader

Compiled by Marlene Peterson

Libraries of Hope

Contents

Chapter 1

❧

David Crockett

1789-1836

David Crockett, by Chester Harding, 1834

A few years before the War of 1812, there was a very homesick little boy in Virginia. His home was only a hut of logs in the wilderness of eastern Tennessee, but the one thing that he wanted most was to see it again. His father had hired him to a drover to help drive some cattle a journey of four hundred miles. So plan was made for his return, but the twelve-year-old boy made one for himself. He soon found that the only means of getting away from the drover was to run away. One stormy night he tramped seven miles through the snow to join a man who was going toward his home; but the man went so slowly that the impatient boy pushed on ahead and made much of the long journey alone.

This was the beginning of his adventures. From that time until he was fifteen he drove cattle, did farm work, and contrived somehow to get enough money together to buy a rifle. When he was fifteen he concluded that he ought to know something of books; so he began to go to school four days in the week, working two days for his board. In six months he learned to read a little, to write his name, and to do easy examples in addition, subtraction, division, and multiplication; and that was all the "schooling" that he ever had. When he was eighteen his property consisted of a snit of coarse homespun, a rifle, and a horse that he had not paid for. The next thing that he did was to get a wife; but it did not seem to occur to him until after the wedding that he had no home for the pretty little girl of seventeen who had married him. They looked about them, found a log cabin that some one had left, and moved in. The bride's parents gave them two cows and two calves. A man for whom David had worked lent them fifteen dollars with which to furnish their house.

One day, three or four years later, David said to his wife, "Let us go to western Tennessee. The land here is all taken up, but there we can have four hundred acres if we build a house and plant some corn." The little wife was willing to go wherever her husband wished and they set out. She and her two little boys rode on the horse. The furs that they used for bedding, their few dishes, and their spinning wheel were put upon the backs of David's two colts; and so the family made a journey of two hundred and fifty miles through the wilderness. Then David built a log house, made a table and some three-legged stools, drove some pegs into the walls to hang their clothes on, if they happened to have any that they were not wearing, and they were at home. David was a remarkably good marksman, and they had plenty of venison and wild turkey. There was a stream at hand that was full of fish. No one need starve in such a place.

But David was restless. In two years he moved again. Then came the War of 1812. There was trouble with the Indians in Alabama, and he volunteered as a soldier. The Indians wished to be friendly, but some rascally white men had been stealing from them and had even shot some of them. At last the Indians began to pay back. They made an attack upon a fort and killed almost every one in it. The whole region was aroused. "I am going to help fight the Indians," said David to his wife.

"But what can we do if they come upon us?" she exclaimed. "We are hundreds of miles from my friends. If anything should happen to you, we should starve."

So she pleaded, but David replied, "I ought to go. I owe it to my country. Moreover, if we do not punish them, they will kill us all." And away he went.

So it was that he became a soldier. He was a great favorite, and no wonder, for he was not only a daring fighter but a good hunter. After a little while the officers said one to another, "We may as well let Crockett do what he pleases, he always comes out right." So after that this independent soldier did just what he chose. He would slip away from the line of march and come back, perhaps with a turkey that he had shot. Even a squirrel was welcome in those hungry days, and whatever David had he was ready to share. No one could help liking him, for he was so generous and so full of fun. Wherever he went there were good times.

David was a strong man, but there came a time when he suddenly became very ill many miles from camp. As he lay under a tree, some Indians came that way. They stopped and looked at him. He had powder and bullets and a rifle, the three things that they cared for most; but, instead of taking them and walking off, they said by signs, "Sick? Eat this;" and they held a piece of melon to his lips. He felt so badly that he could not eat even that. Then one of them said, "You will die and be buried if you do not eat." Another said, "Come, I will go with you and carry your gun;" and they all went with him to the nearest house, a mile and a half away.

He was sick for several weeks, but at last he found his way home. A little later his wife and the youngest child were again on horseback, for now David was going to southern Tennessee. Other settlers came there, some thieves among them. "We must have a justice of the peace," the settlers declared. "Let's take Crockett." So the hunter became a magistrate. He had never read a page of a law book, but he had a good deal of common sense, and he did just what he thought was fair. When a man was accused of stealing anything, this new justice would say, "Catch that fellow and bring him up for trial." Then if he proved to be the thief, Crockett would order, "Tie him up and give him a whipping." By and by Crockett was made a magistrate by law, and now he was in trouble; for he was told that his warrant for arresting men must be in what he called "real writing," and he could hardly scribble his own name. He got over this difficulty by saying to the constable, "Whenever you see that a warrant is necessary, you needn't come all the way to me. Just fill one out, and if it isn't right, I'll change it." Then the justice went to work, and before long he could not only write a warrant but keep his record book.

But he was growing restless again, and soon he made another move. This time he built his cabin seven miles from the nearest neighbor. To this lonely place a man came one day and showed him a newspaper. It said that Crockett was a candidate for the legislature. "They mean that for a joke on me," said Crockett, "but I'll make them pay for it." So he set out to persuade people that he was the one they wanted to help make their laws; and when the time came to vote, David Crockett was elected.

Portrait of Davy Crockett, by John Gadsby Chapman

By and by the backwoodsman and two well-educated men were nominated for Congress. At a meeting Crockett spoke first and then was followed by the other two. They tried to answer each other, but said not a word about Crockett. One of these had been much annoyed while making his speech by some guinea hens, and at last had asked to have them driven away. As soon as he stopped speaking, Crockett called out, "General, you had not the politeness to allude to me in your speech. But when my little friends, the guinea hens, came up and began to holler, 'Crockett, Crockett, Crockett,' you were ungenerous enough to drive them all away." This raised a laugh. When the time came to vote, Crockett was elected; and later he set out in the old stagecoach for Washington.

Now David Crockett could write, but he had learned little more from books. He had, however, learned a good deal from people. He said before he went to the legislature, "If anyone had come along and told me he was 'the government,' I should have believed him." But he had kept his ears open, he had asked questions, and, best of all, he had done a great amount of thinking, and had his own opinion on all questions of the day, General Jackson was the "big man" of his party, and Crockett voted for whatever bills he proposed until one was brought forward that he did not think just. He voted against that one. After his term in Congress was over, he made a little speech, explaining why he had not followed the general. "Gentlemen," he said, "there was once a boy whose master told him to plow across the field to a red cow. Well, he began to plow and she began to walk; and he plowed all the forenoon after her. When the master came, he swore at him for going so crooked. 'Why, sir,' said the boy, 'you told me to plow to the red cow, and I kept after her, but she always kept moving.'"

People liked Crockett not only because he could tell funny stories and make them all laugh, but because he was so honest and truthful and brave; because he had so much common sense and was so reasonable; and because he was so kind and friendly and generous to everyone. He was petted and praised wherever he went. Presents were given him, he was invited to dinners and treated with the utmost honor. Crowds came together to hear him speak, and he was always cheered and applauded.

But now a great disappointment came to the congressman. He had expected to be elected again, and perhaps some day to be made President; but the people who voted for him in the first place were friends of General Jackson, and they would not elect anyone who was against him. Crockett had seen his last days in Congress. He went home and wrote, "Here, like the wearied bird, let me settle down for awhile, and shut out the world." But he was soon uneasy and restless. War was going on with Mexico, and he mounted his horse and rode away to help carry it on. He fought furiously, but finally was taken prisoner. The Mexican President had ordered that all prisoners should be put to death, so David Crockett never returned to the little log house in the Tennessee wilderness.

Chapter 2

ℰℒ

William Travis

1809-1836

The world has heard the name of William B. Travis. The world has heard the story of his heroic life and death. The world is glad to recognize his fair, unspotted fame. The pages of history are brighter because his name is written there, and he was favored among men to have been given the glorious opportunity of dying as he died, a splendid example of unselfish service.

William B. Travis was born in Edgefield County, South Carolina, but he grew to manhood in Alabama. He taught school and studied law in Alabama, and married one of the pretty girls who went to school to him.

The next year after his marriage he left his family in Alabama and came to Texas. Soon after he arrived at Annahuac (An'-a-hac), because he said just exactly what he thought about the haughty, tyrannical Bradhue, the Commander of the Fort, he, with others, was thrown into the bar-racks' prison. After he was released from prison he removed to San Felipe, the capital of the colony. While he was Secretary of the Ajuntimento (A-yoon'-te-myen'-to), in 1834, he drew up a petition praying for the release of General Stephen F. Austin, then confined in prison in the city of Mexico.

Travis, in the spring of 1835, raised a company, captured and disarmed Tenoria, the Mexican officer whom Santa Anna had sent with a squad of troops to guard the post at Annahuac. But these captured men were soon released by the authorities and their arms and papers restored to them.

In 1835, Ugartechea (Oo-gar-ta-

William Barret Travis, by Henry McArdle

5

cha'-a), in command at San Antonio, ordered the arrest of Travis and other Texans. Travis hastened to the west and joined the army under Stephen F. Austin.

With a band of barely one hundred and fifty men, on February the twenty-second, the day that Santa Anna's advance division reached San Antonio, Travis retired to the fortress-church, Alamo, which was strongly defended.

On the twenty-fourth of February he sent out the following announcement:

Commandancy of the Alamo,
Bexar, Feb'y 24th, 1836.

To the People of Texas and all Americans in the World, Fellow Citizens and Compatriots:

I am besieged by a thousand or more of the Mexicans under Santa Anna. I have sustained a continual bombardment and cannonade for 24 hours and have not lost a man. The enemy has demanded a surrender at discretion, otherwise the garrison are to be put to the sword, if the fort is taken. I have answered the demand with a cannon shot, and our flag still waves proudly from the walls. I shall never surrender or retreat. Then, I call on you, in the name of Liberty, of patriotism and everything dear to the American character to come to our aid with all dispatch. The enemy is receiving reinforcements daily and will, no doubt, increase to three or four thousand in four or five days. If this call is neglected, I am determined to sustain myself as long as possible and die like a soldier who never forgets what is due to his own honor and that of his country. Victory or Death.

WILLIAM BARRETT TRAVIS,
Lt. Col. Com'd't.

P.S. The Lord is on our side. When the enemy appeared in sight we had not three bushels of corn. We have since found in deserted houses 80 or 90 bushels and got into the walls 20 or 30 head of beeves.

TRAVIS.

Illustration from *Brief History of Texas* by D.W.C. Baker, 1873

In another letter to a friend in Alabama he said, "Take care of my little boy; if the country is saved I may make him a splendid fortune, if it is lost, and I perish, he will know that he is the son of a man who died for his country."

On March the third, Travis sent a letter to the convention at Washington in which he said, "I am here in fine spirits, with one hundred and forty-five men. I have held the place against a force of from one thousand five hundred to six thousand, and I will continue to hold it until I receive relief from my countrymen, or I will die defending the fort. I know the courage of my men will not fail them in their last struggle. God and Texas! Liberty or Death!"

Chapter 3

ℰ

Remember the Alamo!

1836

Spanish mission of the Alamo, from *The Romance and Tragedy of Pioneer Life* by William Ludwell Sheppard, 1883.

This is the tale of a mission church that became a stone fortress, about which raged a people's struggle for independence. It is a tale of brave men whom it sheltered against the over-whelming power of an army, only to lose their lives at its altars in defense of its sacred walls and liberty.

It was in the year 1836, when Texas was a province of Mexico, and was fighting for its independence. Hemmed in, in a little mission church known as the Alamo, in San Antonio, on the Texas frontier, forty-six brave American frontiersmen faced an army of 4,000 Mexican troops under General Santa Anna. Deceived as to the number of men in the Alamo, Santa Anna feared to make the attack that would have quickly forced their surrender. Instead, he laid siege to the little stone fortress.

Texas was determined to be independent. Mexico, laying claim to the territory, was equally bent upon retaining possession of it. All along the frontier, little bodies of daring pioneers were armed and waiting for the invaders. Had these rugged heroes of the woods and plains worked together, they could easily have driven Santa Anna out of the country. But organization was lacking, and Santa Anna was thus enabled to attack one small band at a time. Colonel William B. Travis, with his garrison of forty-five men, occupied the Alamo, when Santa Anna, with his army of Mexicans, attacked it. With true frontier heroism, they refused to surrender, resolved to die fighting.

Miles away, on the Rio Grande, Davy Crockett, with his little band of 140 sturdy woodsmen, heard that Travis and his men were besieged. Instantly they started to the rescue. It was a long, hard march, but they were trained to such work, and the Alamo was reached before Santa Anna had discovered the weakness of the garrison.

Davy Crockett was a pioneer and a fighter. He had dealt with the Indians, and was educated in the stealthy mode of Indian attack. Now he kept his men concealed, and under the cover of night made a reconnaissance. Then he learned his fatal mistake. He had expected to find the Mexicans numbered by hundreds. Instead, they were numbered by thousands. On all sides of the Alamo they were drawn up, company after company. Even reinforced by his small band, there was no chance for the heroic defenders of the fort. For his men to enter was to go to certain doom.

A short conference was held. Crockett made it plain to his men that, even under the most favorable circumstances, they could not hope to save the handful of men in the mission. The most they could do, was to die with them. Then came the question; "Shall we go in?"

It took but a moment to decide. To a man the answer was the same.

"Yes."

At the break of dawn, when Santa Anna's men were drowsily pacing their beats, Davy Crockett and his band made their rush for the stockade-gate. Taken by surprise, the Mexicans were thrown into confusion, and, before they could rally to oppose the rush, the gateway had been gained. The gates swung open, and Crockett and his men, self-condemned, entered the Alamo, shouting to the cheering defenders, "We've come to die with you!"

With the break of day, Santa Anna again laid siege to the fort. Attack after attack was made, only to be repulsed. The defenders were sure shots. Not a charge of powder was wasted from the inside of the walls, while all day long the bullets pattered against the sides of the fort, now and then finding an entrance through a loop-hole or window, to lodge in the body of one of the defenders,

The Fall of the Alamo, by Robert Jenkins Onderdonk, c. 1903

Death of Crockett, from *Stories of the Great West* by Theodore Roosevelt, 1914

and reduce the garrison by one more. Night came, but the assault still continued. Under the cover of darkness, the Mexicans carried up a ladder and placed it against the outside of the stockade; but to try to gain entrance in that manner was worse than useless. Davy Crockett was there to meet the first man who dared to climb; with knife in hand, he saluted each newcomer, and soon this plan was abandoned.

From then on, the siege was continuous. Night and day the Mexicans stormed the little stockade. Slowly but surely, the slender company of heroes grew smaller and smaller. The losses of the besiegers were ten to one, but still there was no hope. Travis, the brave commander of the little garrison fell, mortally wounded, and the direction of the fight fell to Davy Crockett and Colonel Jim Bowie. Without rest or sleep, the survivors stuck to their places, fighting on and on until they fell. The Mexican dead numbered a thousand. The troops had to be driven to the attack at the point of their officers' swords, and still Davy Crockett and the few survivors fought, knowing it was but to die in the end.

Eleven days passed. Worn to the brink of death from their continuous fighting, the few defenders who remained were failing in their marksmanship. Only the unconquerable courage of Davy Crockett kept them at it. It was not want of courage which ailed them, but simply exhaustion and lack of sleep. Santa Anna, alert for the opportunity, massed his forces in front of the stockade. The little band inside prepared to die. With ladders and battering rams the Mexicans advanced. By the dozen they were shot, but the column never stopped till it reached the wall. The battering-rams crashed against the gate. It yielded and finally opened. Through the gap the Mexicans flooded. In one corner of the stockade the dozen survivors gathered for their last stand.

A small Mexican cannon was hauled into the Alamo. In one room lay the wounded and dying. But now that the end had come, every man who could pull a trigger was a fighter. Travis, dying, unable to move, shot until a sabre-stroke stilled his hand forever. The cannon was dragged to the door of the room where the wounded lay. One discharge, and then a few bayonet-thrusts had finished all but Crockett and five of his men. In a little corner, they battled like demons.

Surrounded by a pile of dead bodies, these five were finally overpowered and taken prisoners. They were led before Santa Anna. Gloating over his victory, which had cost him 1,600 men, the Mexican general promised the dauntless five their safety as prisoners of war. Even as he spoke the words, the five heroes were approached from behind by order of the treacherous general. Crockett, at the sign of bad faith, started to spring at Santa Anna's throat. He was too late. He fell, pierced by twelve swords. Crockett and his brave men had indeed died with the Alamo garrison.

It was from this tragic incident that the war-cry was derived, "Remember the Alamo!"

The Alamo in San Antonio, Texas

Chapter 4

ಐ

Sam Houston

1798-1863

Sam Houston was born at Timber Ridge Church, seven miles from Lexington, Rockbridge County, Virginia, March the second, 1798. His father was a brave soldier in the war of the American Revolution. His mother was a sweet, lovable woman, and had the greatest influence over the life of her son. When other people did not seem to understand his strange ways, she always seemed to know all about it, and she was the first one to find out that her boy had a great heart and a great head.

Young Sam loved to have his own way and he never wanted to take anybody's advice. The neighbors said, "Sam is a headstrong boy and he will never come to a good end." But Sam was learning how to depend upon himself and he did not think he needed their advice.

When his mother was left a widow with six sons and three daughters, and had to sell her old home and move many miles away into a new country, Sam Houston took up work with a will. He took good care of this sweet mother that he loved so much.

Sam Houston, by J.C. Buttre, 1858

Their new home, about eight miles from the Tennessee River, which was then the boundary line between the white people's territory and that of the Cherokee Indians, was near a good school called an academy. Sam liked to go to school fairly well, but there were some studies that he liked very much and some that he did not like at all. The ones that he did not like he refused to study and the ones that he enjoyed he never wanted to put down.

12

One day he told his schoolmaster that he thought he would like to study Latin. The schoolmaster, who probably was busy at the time Sam spoke to him, said, "No, not now." Sam was so disappointed that he turned around and said, "I'll never recite another lesson while I live." But he did not declare that he would never study another lesson while he lived. He became a great reader and he found many good and useful books to read.

There is a wonderful book, Homer's "Iliad," which is a classic, and this book Sam Houston loved to read, and he memorized many passages in it. This great book, which told him about the soldiers of ancient times and the people of deep thought and industry, so entertained and instructed him that he kept a copy of it with him. Often, when he was in camp or away on a long journey, he would sleep with it under his pillow.

His older brothers, who had never read this wonderful book, could not understand why Sam loved it so. They didn't understand Sam, so they said, "Sam, you are a lazy boy and we are going to put you to work." This they did. They put Sam to work in a country store where he had to do a little of everything, sweep out the store, wait on customers, run errands and sometimes drive a mule team.

This boy, who loved to read about the heroes in a book like Homer's "Iliad," could not make himself contented in a country store selling pins and needles and running errands. One day when he heard the roar of the falls at the river and felt the call in his blood to go to the woods, he decided to run away. He loved the Cherokee Indians, and he wanted to leave the store and go to live with them.

Though he ran away from his home and joined the red-skinned men that he loved, he did not forget his mother. He would go home often to see her and tell her all about his travels and the strange things that the Indians did. His mother would mend his clothes and they would have long walks and talks together. His mother, too, loved the animals in the wild woods, and she enjoyed hearing his accounts of the happy days with the Indians. After these short visits to his mother, Sam would hurry back to his wild life in the woods.

Sam wore the Indians' dress, learned their customs, habits, and language, and lived just exactly as they did.

One of the things that interested him very much during these wild days was the study of the Indian character. Sam found out that in order to make his Indian friends true to him, he must be true to them. He learned that an Indian never forgets a kindness, even a small kindness, and that an Indian can love very much, and he would risk his life to help a friend in trouble. He also learned that the Indian knows how to hate, and he feels it his duty to punish his enemies. The Indians understood Sam, too, and he had a place in their hearts if they were savage hearts. Years afterwards when this young runaway boy became President of the Republic of Texas not one Indian ever violated a treaty.

Before he went to live with the Indians he had contracted a few debts which he wanted to earn enough money to pay, so he returned to his home to find some employment. He easily secured a country school and he taught it successfully.

Sam Houston was only nineteen years of age in 1812 when the United States and England were at war, called the War of 1812. He enlisted in the army of the United States at Maryville, Tennessee.

His mother had known since he was a small boy that his greatest desire in life was to be a soldier, so, when he entered the army, she helped him in every way that she could and told him he must always be a brave and true man and never afraid to fight for the right. It was not long before he was made Sergeant, then Ensign, and the officer in command said he was one of the best drilled men in the company. The battle of Tohopeka, which means horseshoe bend, was a fierce bloody battle between the white men and the Indians. In this battle, in which General Andrew Jackson was in command, Sam Houston received a wound from which he suffered the remainder of his life. It was here that Houston won the life-long admiration and friendship of General Jackson.

At the close of this war Houston was appointed Lieutenant of the First Regiment of Infantry and placed at New Orleans. Here his wound was treated, but the suffering that he endured was the kind that can be endured only by those who have nerve and great self-control.

In April, 1816, Houston visited New York and Washington City, and in 1817 he was called for duty to the Adjutant's office at Nashville, Tennessee. After a few months of service in this office he was appointed under-agent among the Cherokee Indians, to carry out a treaty which had been made with the Cherokee nation.

He went with a delegation of Indians to Washington, where he appeared before President Monroe and Secretary of War, John C. Calhoun, making a fine exhibit of what he had done and what he believed to be right. His work for the Indians was approved and appreciated.

Houston soon gave up the Indian agency and his lieutenancy in the army and went to Nashville where he began to study law. He knew much of men and affairs; he had for years been a careful observer of men's hearts and minds, so after six months of study he applied for a license to practice law. He obtained his license and, with a small library, opened a law office in Lebanon, Tennessee.

In that same year, he was elected District Attorney and moved to Nashville. He was appointed Adjutant-General of Tennessee, and in 1821 was elected Major-General by the field officers of the division which represented two-thirds of the State.

He was a successful lawyer and had he continued in the practice of the law, he would have risen to a place with the great lawyers of the country.

He was elected in 1823, without opposition, to a seat in the House of Representatives of the United States, and returned, without opposition, for a second term.

In 1827 he was elected Governor of Tennessee, and no man in Tennessee had more friends or more power than Sam Houston.

One day he suddenly resigned the office of Governor and gave up his public life, all that held out opportunity to him as a lawyer and a statesman, and returned to his home with the Cherokee Indians. The same old chief that had loved him as a runaway, wandering boy, held out his arms to him, opened wide the door of the wigwam and welcomed him lovingly back to his home in the forests.

He was a great help now to his old friends, for he sat at their council fires, gave them advice, and watched with keen eye the wrongs that were put upon them by selfish officials who looked after their own welfare instead of the welfare of the Indians.

Houston went to Washington to see what he could do to help the Indians. With the assistance of General Jackson he had five agents and under-agents removed, and he asked the Government of the United States to look into the Indian affairs, and this the Government did.

Though Houston's friends begged him not to do so, after he had found aid for his red-skinned friends, he went back to their wigwams in the forest to make his home with them.

Sam Houston Comes to Texas

General Jackson requested Houston to confer with the fierce, wild Comanche Indians who were not only feared by the white people but by all of the other Indian tribes. General Jackson knew that Houston understood Indians well and that he had influence over them. He wanted the Comanches to send a delegation to Fort Gibson on the Arkansas river, with the purpose of later visiting Washington City, for he was very anxious that a treaty of peace might be made with this savage tribe. Nothing but this treaty would protect the people who had been so harassed by these Indians.

On December the first, 1832, Houston, with a few companions, left his Indian home on the Arkansas and started for Fort Towson. At Nacogdoches, he told the authorities why he had come into Texas, and he traveled on to San Felipe de Austin, the capital of Austin's colony. From here, in accord with General Jackson's plan, he traveled to San Antonio de Bexar, where he carried out the plan of the treaty with the Comanches.

Sam Houston had been watching affairs in Texas, the Mexican cruelties and oppression, and the almost helpless condition of the Texans. He deeply sympathized with the Texans. He boldly made up his mind to help Texas fight for her freedom.

When he returned to Nacogdoches he was notified that he had been elected a delegate to the convention to be held at San Felipe in April, 1833.

This was the convention that decided to send a request to the government of Mexico to repeal their cruel, oppressive laws, and Stephen F. Austin carried the request or memorial.

Mexico refused to change her laws, she became more and more cruel, and the Texans said they would wait no longer, but would resist her by force.

All of the forces in Texas were brought together and Sam Houston was made Commander-in-Chief of the army of Texas. On March the second, 1836, Sam Houston's birthday, the Independence of Texas was declared at Washington on the Brazos. General Houston gathered the forces between the Brazos and the Guadalupe, while Santa Anna, at the head of a strong army of Mexican soldiers, in three divisions, was advancing from the West. With what forces he could gather, he retreated before the main division of Santa Anna's army, while his scouts constantly reported the movements of the enemy.

Houston was sure that Santa Anna would follow him to the head of the San Jacinto river, so he marched to that point. By cutting off all means of escape, he determined to win or die. Houston moved so slowly that the Texas soldiers became alarmed. Even those who trusted him most grew impatient, and murmured at the delays in their onward march. He began to retreat March the thirteenth, traveling slowly from Gonzales to the Colorado, thence to the several points on the Brazos, with Santa Anna's army close behind. Men, women and children were fleeing at the very sound of Santa Anna's name. So strange did General Houston's movements seem to the people that they began to wonder, in terror, if they were going to be protected by the Texas army.

In the meantime, Santa Anna, feeling very proud of his recent victories, and sure that he would have others, had allowed the three divisions of his army to scatter. The so-called central division, which he accompanied in person, commanded by Generals Sesma and Filisola, had been following Houston upon his retreat. So sure did Santa Anna feel of his power over the Texans that he left his main army on the Brazos, and with about one thousand men went to Harrisburg. Here he thought he could capture President Burnet and his cabinet. He found Harrisburg deserted, so he burned the town and marched rapidly to New Washington; which town he also burned. It was his plan to follow the President and his cabinet to New Washington, take them prisoners, and declare the war at an end.

But while his army was getting ready to take the ferry at Lynchburg (Lynch's Ferry) a scout reported to Santa Anna that Houston and the Texas army were near at hand. This information took Santa Anna, who was separated from his army, by surprise.

As the Texans prepared for battle, they neglected nothing, not even the smallest detail, and they obeyed every command of their chieftain. The day was fine, and after each Texan had eaten his simple breakfast, General Houston looked over his army. He encouraged the soldiers by his cheerful words, and by telling each officer what he wanted him to do. He told "Deaf" Smith, a cool-headed scout, to get two good axes and hide them in a safe place, easy to reach, where, upon a moment's notice, he could bring them out for use. He told Smith not to pass the sentinel's lines without notice from him.

A large force had arrived to join Santa Anna, and there was much moving and stirring in the Mexicans' camp. General Houston knew the effect this would have upon his men. He told them that what looked like new forces for the enemy were the same Mexicans they had seen the day before, who were just marching up and down in order to frighten the Texas soldiers, and that it was a way the Mexicans had of alarming the Texans.

At this same time, General Houston sent "Deaf" Smith and one comrade with secret orders to go to the rear of that new Mexican force to find out how large it was, then return quietly to him.

When the messengers returned they reported where the soldiers could hear, "That it was just as the General had said, the Mexicans were only trying to frighten the Texans." But to the General's ear they whispered that "General Cos had come by forced marches with more than five hundred men to reinforce Santa Anna."

General Houston immediately called a council of his field officers, under the solemn oaks at San Jacinto, and the council determined upon battle.

Seeing that the Texans were restless and eager for attack, General Houston called "Deaf" Smith and his companions to him, and he went with them to the place where the axes had been hid that morning. Handing an axe to each of these reliable men the General said, "Take these axes, make your way to Vinces Bridge, cut it down and come back like eagles or you will lose the day."

The cutting down of Vinces bridge, across Vinces bayou, a stream which empties into Buffalo bayou, stopped all chance of escape, for both armies had had to cross it to reach the battle ground.

At three o'clock in the afternoon of April the twenty-first, 1836, General Houston made the charge which inspired every Texan. "Remember the Alamo!" and "Remember Goliad!" rang out the voices of the Texans. The Mexicans, who were either taking their afternoon nap or hiding behind trees and bushes, were completely taken by surprise. At this moment, "Deaf" Smith rode up, his horse covered with mire and foam, shouting, as he waved his axe over his head, "I have cut down Vinces Bridge! Fight for your lives and remember the Alamo!"

The mounted Texas soldiers were first sent to the front, advancing in steady lines, and the cannon was carried within two hundred yards of the enemy's breast-works.

The two cannon "Twin sisters," a gift of the city of Cincinnati to the Republic of Texas, kept up a steady firing, shattering and shivering everything they struck. As General Houston spurred his horse into the very breast of the foe, the Texans rushed solidly upon the Mexicans. The Mexicans, lined up in exact order, sent a heavy storm of bullets, but sent them too high, and they went over the heads of the Texans.

General Houston was wounded in the ankle and his horse was shot. When they had used all of their ammunition, the Texans used their rifles as war clubs. After firing one shot from their pistols the Texans did not stop to re-load, but threw the heavy iron at the head of some Mexican. Like wild men the Texans flew after the Mexicans who tried to escape.

In no sense did the Mexicans show a lack of courage and readiness upon the field of San Jacinto. They made bold charges, but, as the battle advanced, they began to realize what their massacres at Goliad and at the Alamo meant to the Texans.

When the last line of Texans was charged by a Mexican division, General Houston dashed to the front of his men, shouting, "Come on, my brave fellows, your General leads you!" The right and left wings of the Mexican army had been scattered before the central portion was broken, but soon the Mexican soldiers, each one bent on saving his life, staggered or fell in the oozy, swampy grass.

When the flying Mexicans, pursued by the Texans, reached Vinces Bayou, and found that the bridge was gone, they clung to the banks, or plunged into the dark, muddy water, sinking to the bottom. The few who succeeded in crossing fell back into the water, shot by some Texan.

As a last means of escape some of the Mexicans had rushed to the island of green trees where the Mexicans had been in camp. Here the marshy ground was deep, and the horses, with their riders, sank into the mire and were instantly covered over. Dead men, horses, saddles, guns, pistols, soon made a bridge over the marshy ground.

Almonte, secretary to Santa Anna, and some of his men had agreed that they would either fight the Texans or surrender, but that they would not run away. General Houston, with as many men as he could gather together, led them to a charge, but his wounded horse fell dead with seven bullets in his faithful body. Not until his horse fell did the Texans know that General Houston was wounded. As his wounded leg touched the ground, he fell. He gave his command to General Rusk and another horse was brought to him.

As General Rusk advanced upon the Mexicans, Almonte came forward with his sword. The Alamo and Goliad were remembered and San Jacinto was won!

Santa Anna was captured by the Texans and was a prisoner at their mercy. On the morning of the twenty-second of April he was taken, by the Texas soldiers to General Houston, who, on account of the pain from his wound, lay upon a blanket under a tree.

Santa Anna bowed very low, and, with fine words, began the interview.

"I am General Antonio Lopez de Santa Anna, a prisoner of war, sir, at your disposal."

General Houston asked him to be seated. Santa Anna continued, "Sir, you should be very considerate, for, remember, you have captured the Napoleon of the West."

"Do you expect mercy at *our* hands when *you* showed none at the Alamo?" asked General Houston.

To this inquiry Santa Anna replied, "When a fort refuses to surrender, and is taken by assault, the prisoners are doomed to death, according to the rules of war."

"If that be true," replied Houston, "such a rule is a disgrace to this civilized nineteenth century.

Tell me, sir," continued Houston, "under what rule of war do you place Goliad?"

To this Santa Anna replied, "I had orders from my government to execute every man taken with arms in his hands."

"Ah, sir," replied Houston, "*you are the government*, for *you* are *Dictator!* Who, in your government, can be superior to you, who are *Dictator?* You must, at once, write an order for all Mexican troops to abandon our country and return to their homes."

Had there been a way out of this, Santa Anna would have found it, but there was no escape from him here. He wrote the order and it was sent by "Deaf" Smith and Henry Karnes to General Filisola, who was second in command.

Santa Anna tried to discuss with General Houston the matter of purchasing his freedom but the Texan Commander told him that such matters must come before the government of Texas.

Some of the Texans thought that Santa Anna's own blood ought to pay the price of his treatment of the Texans, but General Houston decided upon another course. His dealings with Santa Anna were tactfully made and showed his great sense. He formed a solid compact with Santa Anna which provided that he should never again take up arms against the Texans. Every Mexican soldier was to be sent home. All property, great or small, valuable or not, which the Mexicans had captured from the Texans, should be returned.

Portrait of General Sam Houston, by Mathew Brady, 1861

Santa Anna solemnly promised to abide by the terms of this compact. President Burnet detained Santa Anna a prisoner for a time, but he was liberated by General Houston and sent to New Washington in July, 1837, and from there he returned to Mexico.

Houston's Further Service to Texas

At the next election for President, General Sam Houston with great rejoicing was chosen the first constitutional President of the Republic of Texas. He was elected at Columbia on the Brazos, then the Capital of Texas. He served one term in the Texas Congress and from 1841 to 1845 he again served the Republic of Texas as President.

President Houston was anxious for Texas to become one of the States in the United States. When Texas was admitted into the Union in 1845 he was elected to the United States Senate, serving until May, 1857.

In 1857, Runnels defeated Houston for Governor of Texas, and in 1859 Houston defeated Runnels for the same office.

In 1861, when war between the northern and the southern states began, many of the southern States left the Union. The Texas people wanted their State to leave the Union for they believed in all of the principles taught by the South. For the first time, the people of Texas would not listen to Houston who did not want Texas to leave the Union.

In January, 1861, a convention sat at Austin, Texas, which considered whether or not Texas should leave the Union. Houston would not attend the convention.

On February the twenty-third, 1861, the matter was submitted to the people of the State.

As Governor Houston was honestly opposed to Texas leaving the Union and as the people wanted their State to withdraw, they declared his office vacant. Some of his friends wanted to sustain him in office but he saw the results which might come by force, so he quietly gave the office up.

Though the people did not, at the time, agree with Houston, he could look far ahead and see what they could not see. He knew the conditions in both the north and the south, and some of the things that he said "would certainly happen" came about exactly as he said they would.

Though Texas, against Houston's will, left the Union, he always loved her, and one of his sons, with Houston's consent, served in the Confederate Army.

Sam Houston's last days were spent at his home in Huntsville. On Sunday, June the twenty-sixth, 1863, surrounded by his family, his bold, fine spirit went back to God.

His remains rest at Huntsville, under a tomb which, in accord with an act of the Texas Legislature, has been placed there by the people of Texas.

The beautiful city of Houston, situated on Buffalo Bayou, twenty-two miles from the San Jacinto battlefield, is named for General Sam Houston.

The State of Texas has converted the San Jacinto battle-field into a beautiful park. Broad drive ways, parks and a picturesque boat landing make of this historic spot a very attractive place to visit.

In the words of General Andrew Jackson, which significant phrase is engraved upon the tomb of General Houston:

"The world will take care of Houston's fame."

Sam Houston Monument in Hermann Park, Houston

19

Chapter 5

ജ

How the Mormons Came to Settle Utah

1847

In the winter of 1838-39 a large number of people moved into the country on the east bank of the Mississippi River in the state of Illinois. They had taken the name of "Latter-Day Saints," but were generally called Mormons, and were followers of a new religion that had been founded by a man named Joseph Smith a few years earlier. This strange new religion had attracted many people to it, and the greater number of them had first moved to Ohio, and then into the new state of Missouri, but they were not well received by the people of either of those states, and had finally been driven from Missouri at the point of the sword. Fortunately for them there was plenty of unoccupied land in the West, and their leader decided to take refuge near the town of Quincy in Illinois. At that time a man had only to reside in the state for six months in order to cast a vote for president, and as an election was near at hand the politicians of Illinois were glad to welcome the Mormons. Looking about, the newcomers found two "paper" cities, or places that had been mapped out on paper with streets and houses, but had never actually been built. The Mormon leaders bought two large farms in the "paper" town of Commerce, and many thousand acres in the country adjoining, and there they laid out their new city, to which they gave the strange name of Nauvoo.

The Mormon city lay along the Mississippi River, and its streets and public buildings were planned on a large scale. People flocked to the place, and as the Mormon missionaries were eager workers, the number of converts grew rapidly. A temple was built, which a stranger who saw it in 1843 said was the wonder of the world. Many Mormon emigrants came from England, usually by ship to New Orleans, and thence by river steamboat up the Mississippi to Nauvoo. By the end of 1844 at least fifteen thousand people had settled there, and as many more were scattered through the country in the immediate neighborhood. Nauvoo was the largest city in Illinois, and its only rival in that part of the West was St. Louis. Joseph Smith had obtained a charter, and both the political parties, the Whigs and the Democrats, were doing their best to make friends of his people. Nauvoo had little of the rough look of most newly-settled frontier towns, and handsome houses and public buildings sprang up rapidly along its fine wide streets.

Unfortunately for the Mormons their leader was a man who made enemies as easily as he made friends. He had aroused much ill feeling when he lived in Missouri. As a result, when, one day in May, 1842, Governor Boggs of Missouri was shot and seriously wounded while sitting at the window of his home, many people laid the crime to Smith or his followers, and believed that the prophet himself, as Smith was called, had ordered the shooting. The officers of Missouri asked the governor of Illinois to hand Smith over to them. This was not done, and consequently ill feeling against the prophet grew stronger. In the meantime a man named John C. Bennett, who had joined the Mormons at Nauvoo, and had been the first mayor of the city, deserted the church, and turned into one of the most bitter of its enemies. He denounced the Mormons in letters he wrote to the newspapers, and exposed what he called their secrets. This led other people to attack the ideas of the Mormons, and it was not long before there was almost as much dislike of them in Illinois as there had been in Missouri.

Even in the Mormon church itself there were men who would not agree with all the prophet Joseph Smith said. A few of these men set up a printing-press and published a paper that they called the Nauvoo Expositor. Only one issue of this sheet appeared, dated June 7, 1844. That was enough, however, to raise the wrath of Joseph Smith and his elders, and they ordered the city marshal to destroy the press. The marshal broke the press and type in the main street of the city, and burned the contents of the newspaper office.

The editors hastily fled to the neighboring town of Carthage. The people there and in all the neighboring villages denounced the destruction of the press, and declared that the time had come to force the Mormons to obey the laws, and, if they would not do so, to drive them out of Illinois. Military companies were formed, cannon were sent for, and the governor of the state was asked to call out the militia.

The governor went to the scene of the trouble to investigate. He found all that part of the east shore of the Mississippi divided between the Mormons and their enemies. He ordered the mayor of Nauvoo to send Mormons to him to explain why they had destroyed the printing-press, and when he had heard their story the governor told them that Smith and his elders must surrender to him, or the whole military force of the state would be called out to capture them. But the prophet had not been idle. He had put his city under martial law, had formed what was called the Legion of the Mormons, and had called in his followers from the near-by villages. He had meant to defend his new city; but when he heard the governor's threat to arrest him, he left Nauvoo with a few comrades and started for the Rocky Mountains. Friends went after him, and begged him not to desert his people. He could not resist their appeal to him to return, and he went back, although he was afraid of the temper of his enemies. As soon as he returned to Illinois he was arrested on the charge of treason and of putting Nauvoo under martial law, and together with his brother Hyrum was sent to the jail at Carthage.

Some seventeen hundred men, members of the militia, had gathered at the towns of Carthage and Warsaw, and the enemies of the Mormons urged the governor to march at the head of these troops to Nauvoo. He knew that in the excited state of affairs there was danger that if these troops entered the city they might set it on fire and destroy much property. He therefore ordered all except three companies to disband; with one company he set out to visit the Mormon city, and the other two companies he left to guard the jail at Carthage.

The governor marched to Nauvoo, spoke to the citizens, and, having assured them that he meant no harm to their church, left about sundown on his road back to Carthage. In the meantime, however, events had been happening in the latter place that were to affect the whole history of the Mormons.

The two Smiths, Joseph and Hyrum, with two friends, Willard Richards and John Taylor, were sitting in a large room in the Carthage jail when a number of men, their faces blackened in disguise, came running up the stairway. The door of the room had no lock or bolt, and, as the men inside feared some attack, Hyrum Smith and Richards leaped to the door and shutting it stood with their shoulders against it. The men outside could not force the door open, and began to shoot through it. The two men at the door were driven back, and on the second volley of shot Hyrum Smith was killed. As his brother fell, the prophet seized a six shooting revolver that one of their visitors had left on the table, and going to the door opened it a few inches. He snapped each barrel at the men on the stair; three barrels missed fire, but each of the three that exploded wounded a man. As the prophet fired, Taylor and Richards stood close beside him, each armed with a hickory cane. When Joseph Smith stopped shooting the enemy fired another volley into the room. Taylor tried to strike down some of the guns that were leveled through the broken door.

"That's right, Brother Taylor, parry them off as well as you can!" cried Joseph Smith. He ran to the window, intending to leap out, but as he jumped two bullets fired through the doorway struck him, and also another aimed from outside the building. As soon as the mob saw that the prophet was killed they scattered, alarmed at what had been done.

The people of Carthage and the neighboring country expected that the Legion of the Mormons would immediately march on them and destroy them. Families fled in wagons, on horseback, and on foot. Most of the people of the near-by town of Warsaw crossed the Mississippi in order to put

Exterior of Carthage Jail, by C.C.A. Christensen, 19th Century

Saints Driven from Jackson County Missouri, by C.C.A. Christensen, 19th Century

the river between them and their enemies. In this state of excitement the governor did not know which party to trust, so he rode to the town of Quincy, forty miles away, and at a safe distance from the scene of trouble. But the Mormons made no attempt to avenge the death of their leader; they intended to let the law look after that.

Week by week, however, it grew harder for them to live on friendly terms with the other people of Western Illinois, and more and more troubles arose to sow distrust. The Gentiles, as those who were not Mormons were called, began to charge the Mormons with stealing their horses and cattle, and the state repealed the charter that had been granted to the city of Nauvoo.

During that summer of 1845, the troubles of Nauvoo's people increased. One night in September a meeting of Gentiles at the town of Green Plains was fired on, and many laid the attack to the Mormons. Whether this was true or not, their enemies gathered in force and scoured the country, burning the houses, barns, and crops of the Latter-Day Saints, and driving them from the country behind the walls of Nauvoo. From their city streets the saints rode out to pay their enemies in kind, and so the warfare went on until the governor appointed officers to try to settle the feud. The people, however, wanted the matter settled in only one way. They insisted that the Mormons must leave Illinois. In reply word came from Nauvoo that the Saints would go in the spring, provided that they were not molested, and that the Gentiles would help them to sell or rent their houses and farms, and give them oxen, horses, wagons, dry-goods, and cash in exchange for their property. The

23

Crossing the Mississippi on the Ice, by C.C.A. Christensen, c. 1878

Gentile neighbors would not promise to buy the goods the Mormons had for sale, but promised not to interfere with their selling whatever they could. At last the trouble seemed settled. Brigham Young, the new leader of the Mormons, said that the whole church would start for some place beyond the Rocky Mountains in the spring, if they could sell enough goods to make the journey there. So the people of Nauvoo prepared to abandon the buildings of their new flourishing city on the Mississippi, and spent the winter trading their houses for flour, sugar, seeds, tents, wagons, horses, cattle, and whatever else might be needed for the long trip across the plains.

The Mormons now looked forward eagerly to their march to a new home, and many of them traveled through the near-by states, buying horses and mules, and more went to the large towns in the neighborhood to work as laborers and so add to the funds for their journey. The leaders announced that a company of young men would start west in March, and choose a good situation for their new city. There they would build houses, and plant crops which should be ready when the rest of the Mormons arrived. But they knew there was always a chance that the people of the country would attack them, and therefore they sent messengers to the governors of the territories they would cross, asking for protection on the march. On February 10th Brigham Young and a few other men crossed the Mississippi and selected a spot on Sugar Creek as the first camp for the people who were to follow. Young and the twelve elders of the Mormons traveled together, and wherever their camp was pitched that place was given the name of "Camp of Israel."

The emigrants had a test of hardship even when they first moved across the Mississippi. The temperature dropped to twenty degrees below zero, and the canvas-covered wagons and tents were a poor shelter from the snow-storms for women and children who had been used to the comforts of a large town. Many crossed the Mississippi on ice. When they were gathered on Sugar Creek Brigham Young spoke to them from a wagon. He told them of the perils of the journey, and then called for a show of hands by those who were willing to start upon it; every hand was raised. On March 1st the camp was broken up, and the long western march began. The Mormons were divided into companies of fifty or sixty wagons, and every night the cattle were carefully rounded up and guards set to protect them from attack. From time to time they built more elaborate camps, and men were left in charge to plant grain, build log cabins, dig wells, and fence the farms, in order that they might give food and shelter to other Mormons who would be making the journey later. The weather was all against their progress. Until May it was bitter cold, and there were heavy snow-storms, constant rains, sleet, and thick mud to be fought with, but like many other bands of American pioneers the Mormons pushed resolutely on, some days marching one mile, some days six, until May 16th, when they reached a charming spot on a branch of the Grand River, and built a camp that they called "Mount Pisgah." Here they plowed and planted several acres of land. While this camp was being pitched, Brigham Young and some of the other leaders went on to Council Bluffs and at a place north of Omaha, now the town of Florence, located the last permanent camp of the expedition.

The trail of the Mormons now stretched across all the western country. At each of the camps men, women, and children were living, resting and preparing supplies to cover the next stage of

Leaving Missouri, by C.C.A. Christensen, c. 1878

their journey. But in spite of the care with which the march was planned those who left Nauvoo last suffered the most. There was a great deal of sickness among them, and owing to illness they were often forced to stop for several days at some unprotected point on the prairies. Twelve thousand people in all shared that Mormon march.

The Gentiles in Illinois did not think that the Mormons were leaving Nauvoo as rapidly as they should. Every week from two to five hundred Mormon teams crossed the ferry into Iowa, but the neighbors thought that many meant to stay. Ill feeling against them grew, and a meeting at Carthage called on people to arm and drive out all Mormons who remained by mid-June. Six hundred men armed, ready to march against Nauvoo.

When the Mormons first announced that they meant to leave their prosperous city in Illinois men came hurrying from other parts of the country to pick up bargains in houses and farms that they thought they would find there. Many of these new citizens were as much alarmed at the threats of the neighbors as were the Mormons themselves; some of them armed, and asked the governor to send them aid. The men at Carthage grew very much excited, and started to march on Nauvoo. Word came, however, that the sheriff, with five hundred men, had entered the city, prepared to defend it, and the Gentile army retreated. A few weeks afterward the hostilities broke out again, and seven hundred men with cannon took the road to the city.

Those of the Mormons who were left, a few hundreds in number, had built rude breastworks for protection; some of the Gentile army took these, and the rest marched through the corn fields, and entered the city on another side. A battle followed between the Gentiles in the streets and the Mormons in their houses, and lasted an hour before the Gentiles withdrew to their camp in the corn fields.

Peaceful citizens now tried to settle the matter. They arranged that all the Mormons should leave immediately, and promised to try to protect them from any further attacks. So matters stood until May 17th, when the sheriff and his men marched into the city, and found the last of the Mormons waiting to leave by the ferry. The next day they were told to go at once, and to make sure that they did, bands of armed men went through the streets, broke into houses, threw what goods were left out of doors and windows, and actually threatened to shoot the people. The few remaining Saints, most of them those who had been too ill to take up the march earlier, were now thoroughly frightened, and before sundown the last one of them had fled across the Mississippi. A few days later this last party, six hundred and forty in number, began the long wearisome journey to the far west, and the empty city of Nauvoo was at last in the hands of the Gentiles.

The object of the Mormons was to find a place where they might be free to live according to their own beliefs. So far they had been continually hunting for what they called their own City of Zion. As they spent that winter of 1846-47 in their camp near Council Bluffs, they tried to decide where they would be safest from persecution. The far west had few settlements as yet, and they were free to take what land they would, but the Mormons wanted a site on which to lay the foundations of a city that should one day be rich and prosperous. They decided to send out a party of explorers, and in April, 1847, one hundred and forty-three men, under command of Brigham Young, with seventy-three wagons filled with food and farm tools, left the headquarters to go still farther west. They journeyed up the north fork of the Platte River, and in the valleys found great herds of buffaloes, so many in number that they had to drive them away before the wagons could pass. Each day the bugle woke the camp about five o'clock in the morning. At seven the journey began. The wagons were driven two abreast by men armed with muskets. They were always prepared for attacks from Indians, but in the whole of their long journey no red men ever disturbed them. Each night the wagons were drawn up in a half-circle on the river bank, and the cattle driven into this shelter. At nine the bugle sent them all to bed. So they made their way over the Uinta range to Emigration Canyon. Down this canyon they moved, and presently came to a terrace from which they saw wide

Entering the Great Salt Lake Valley, by C.C.A. Christensen, 19th Century

plains, watered by broad rivers, and ahead a great lake filled with little islands. Three days later the company camped on the plain by the bank of one of the streams, and decided that this should be the site of their new city. They held a meeting at which they dedicated the land with religious ceremonies, and at once set to work to lay off fields and start plowing and planting. Some of them visited the lake, which they called the Great Salt Lake, and bathed in its buoyant waters. Day by day more of the pioneers arrived, and by the end of August they had chosen the site of their great temple, built log cabins and adobe huts, and christened the place the "City of the Great Salt Lake." This name was later changed to Salt Lake City.

It took some time for this large body of emigrants to build their homes. Wood was scarce and had to be hauled over bad roads by teams that were still worn out by the long march, therefore many built houses of adobe bricks, and as they did not know how to use this clay the rains and frost caused many of the walls to crumble, and when snow fell the people stretched cloths under their roofs to protect themselves from the dripping bricks. Many families lived for months in their wagons. They would take the top part from the wheels, and setting it on the ground, divide it into small bedrooms. The furniture was of the rudest sort; barrels or chests for tables and chairs, and bunks built into the side of the house for beds. But at last they were free from their enemies in this distant country. Men in Ohio, Missouri, and Illinois had hounded them from their settlements, but in this far-off region they had no neighbors except a few pioneer settlers, and wandering bands of Indians, who were glad to trade with them. A steady stream of converts to the Mormon church followed that first trail across the plains. A missionary sent to England brought many men and women from that country to the city on the Great Salt Lake. Brigham Young and the other leaders encouraged their followers above all else to cultivate the land. Most of the Mormons were farmers, and what shops there were dealt only in the necessities of life. Food was a matter of the first importance, and they had to rely entirely upon their own efforts to provide it. Every one was given a piece of land for his house, and most of them had their own farms in the outlying country. When they were sure of their food they began to build their temple and other public buildings, and these, like their streets, were all planned on the lines of a great future city. They first called their territory Deseret, but later changed it to the Indian name of Utah.

Salt Lake City, and the territory of Utah, of which it was the chief settlement, might have remained for years almost unknown to the rest of the United States had not gold been discovered in California in the winter of 1849. The news of untold riches in the land that lay between Utah and the Pacific Ocean brought thousands of fortune hunters across the plains, and many of them traveled by way of Salt Lake City. That rush of men brought trade in its track and served to make the Mormons' capital well known. The quest for gold opened up the lands along the Pacific and helped to tie the far west to the rest of the nation. Soon railroads began to creep into the valleys beyond the Rocky Mountains, and wherever they have gone they have brought men closer together. But in Utah the Mormons were the first settlers, and no one could come and drive them out of their chosen land. At last they had found a city entirely of their own. They had not been allowed to live in Nauvoo, and so they built a new capital. Like all founders of new religions the Mormons had to weather many storms, but after they had passed through cold, hunger, and hardships of many kinds they came to their promised land.

Such is the story of the founding of Salt Lake City, the home of the Mormon people.

Chapter 6

❧

Finding Gold in California

1849

California once belonged to Mexico. Then there was a war between this country and Mexico. This is what we call the Mexican War. During that war the United States took California away from Mexico. It is now one of the richest and most beautiful States in the Union. In the old days, when California belonged to Mexico, it was a quiet country. Nearly all the white people spoke Spanish, which is the language of Mexico. They lived mostly by raising cattle. In those days people did not know that there was gold in California. A little gold had been found in the southern part of the State, but nobody expected to find valuable gold mines. A few people from the United States had settled in the country. They also raised cattle.

Some time after the United States had taken California, peace was made with Mexico. California then became a part of our country. About the time that this peace was made, something happened which made a great excitement all over the country. It changed the history of our country, and changed the business of the whole world. Here is the story of it:

A man named Sutter had moved from Missouri to California. He built a house which was called Sutter's Fort. It was where the city of Sacramento now stands. Sutter had many horses and oxen, and he owned thousands of acres of land. He traded with the Indians, and carried on other kinds of business.

But everything was done in the slow Mexican way. When he wanted boards, he sent men to saw them out by hand. It took two men a whole day to saw up a log so as to make a dozen boards. There was no sawmill in all California.

When Sutter wanted to grind flour or meal, this also was done in the Mexican way. A large stone roller was run over a flat stone. But at last Sutter thought he would have a grinding mill of the American sort. To build this, he needed boards. He thought he would first build a sawmill. Then he could get boards quickly for his grinding mill, and have lumber to use for other things.

Sutter sent a man named Marshall to build his sawmill. It was to be built forty miles away from Sutter's Fort. The mill had to be where there were trees to saw.

Marshall was a very good carpenter, who could build almost anything. He had some men working with him. After some months they got the mill done. This mill was built to run by water.

But when he started it, the mill did not run well. Marshall saw that he must dig a ditch below the great water wheel, to carry off the water. He hired wild Indians to dig the ditch.

When the Indians had partly dug this ditch, Marshall went out one January morning to look at it. The clear water was running through the ditch. It had washed away the sand, leaving the pebbles bare. At the bottom of the water Marshall saw something yellow. It looked like brass. He put his

Miners in the Sierras, by Charles Christian Nahl, 1852

hand down into the water and took up this bright, yellow thing. It was about the size and shape of a small pea. Then he looked, and found, another pretty little yellow bead at the bottom of the ditch.

Marshall trembled all over. It might be gold. But he remembered that there is another yellow substance that looks like gold. It is called "fool's gold." He was afraid he had only found fool's gold.

Marshall knew that if it was gold it would not break easily. He laid one of the pieces on a stone; then he took another stone and hammered it. It was soft, and did not break. If it had broken to pieces, Marshall would have known that it was not gold.

In a few days the men had dug up about three ounces of the yellow stuff. They had no means of making sure it was gold.

Then Marshall got on a horse and set out for Sutter's Fort, carrying the yellow metal with him. He traveled as fast as the rough road would let him. He rode up to Sutter's in the evening, all spattered with mud.

He told Captain Sutter that he wished to see him alone. Marshall's eyes looked wild, and Sutter was afraid that he was crazy. But he went to a room with him. Then Marshall wanted the door locked. Sutter could not think what was the matter with the man.

The Cradle, by Henry Sandham, 1883

When he was sure that nobody else would come in, Marshall poured out in a heap on the table the little yellow beads that he had brought.

Sutter thought it was gold, but the men did not know how to tell whether it was pure or not. At last they hunted up a book that told how heavy gold is. Then they got a pair of scales and weighed the gold, putting silver dollars in the other end of the scales for weights. Then they held one end of the scales under water and weighed the gold. By finding how much lighter it was in the water than out of the water, they found that it was pure gold.

All the men at the mill promised to keep the secret. They were all digging up gold when not working in the mill. As soon as the mill should be done, they were going to wash gold.

But the secret could not be kept. A teamster who came to the mill was told about it. He got a few grains of the precious gold.

When the teamster got back to Sutter's Fort, he went to a store to buy a bottle of whisky, but he had no money. The storekeeper would not sell to him without money. The teamster then took out some grains of gold. The storekeeper was surprised. He let the man have what he wanted. The teamster would not tell where he got the gold. But after he had taken two or three drinks of the whisky, he was not able to keep his secret. He soon told all he knew about the finding of gold at Sutter's Mill.

The news spread like fire in dry grass. Men rushed to the mill in the mountains to find gold. Gold was also found at other places. Merchants in the towns of California left their stores. Mechanics laid down their tools, and farmers left their fields, to dig gold. Some got rich in a few weeks. Others were not so lucky.

Soon the news went across the continent. It traveled also to other countries. More than one hundred thousand men went to California the first year after gold was found, and still more poured in the next year. Thousands of men went through the Indian country with wagons. Of course, there were no railroads to the west in that day.

Millions and millions of dollars' worth of gold was dug. In a short time California became a rich State. Railroads were built across the country. Ships sailed on the Pacific Ocean to carry on the trade of this great State. Every nation of the earth had gold from California.

And it all started from one little, round, yellow bead of gold, that happened to lie shining at the bottom of a ditch, on a cold morning not so very long ago.

California Miner with a Pack Horse, by Henry Raschen

Chapter 7

&

The Start of the Civil War

1861

As soon as the election of Lincoln was announced, men of extreme views at the South proceeded at once to carry out their threats of attempting to withdraw from the Union. Seven States seceded, at intervals more or less brief, from the Union, and organized what was known as the Southern Confederacy. Four States seceded later. The people at the North were amazed at the rapidity with which the organization against the national government established itself. The humiliating events of that dread winter of 1860-61 are a part of our history. The government at Washington stood as if paralyzed. The President was a weak, old man, and did not know what to do. Most of his cabinet officers were friendly to the South, and took advantage of their official positions to allow the enemies

Evening Gun, Fort Sumter, by Conrad Wise Chapman & John Gadsby Chapman, 1864

33

Major Anderson Raising the Flag on…Fort Sumter, by Edwin White, 1862

of the country to take possession of the national stores, arms, arsenals, forts, and navy yards, within the limits of the seceding States. The government did not even dare to send reinforcements to the forts along the southern seacoast lest such action should precipitate a civil war. This weak and irresolute action gave the seceding States ample opportunity to prepare for the coming strife at the expense of the nation. This cost the country many millions of dollars and thousands of lives to regain during the next four years.

Such, briefly, was the condition of the country when Abraham Lincoln, fearful of life, came to Washington in March, 1861, and quietly took the reins of the government. How little could the good President, or even the wisest of his advisers, realize the overwhelming responsibility of his position.

With the stirring events which followed we are familiar. The story of how Major Anderson removed his little band of United States troops from Fort Moultrie to Fort Sumter, in Charleston harbor, for greater safety, is a familiar one; likewise, how the Confederates fired upon a vessel sent with supplies intended for it; and, finally, after a severe bombardment, how they compelled the fort to surrender. Forbearance had ceased to be a virtue. It was seen even by the most timid and conservative that something must be done at once to assert the majesty and power of the national government. President Lincoln acted resolutely and promptly. On the 15th of April, 1861, he issued a proclamation calling out seventy-five thousand militia, for three months, to suppress the rebellion.

The people of the North answered promptly and vigorously to the dry and formal words of the proclamation. No one had suspected how deep in the hearts of the people was the sentiment of patriotism. The lowering of the flag at Fort Sumter pierced the pride and the honor of the North to the quick. The morning and evening of a single day saw peace utterly laid aside, and twenty millions of people filled with the spirit of war.

The same scenes were at the same time occurring in the Southern States. Even more fiery was the outbreak, because the people were of more demonstrative natures.

And thus it came to pass that thirty millions of people, divided into two bands, went seeking each other through the darkness and mystery of war.

Chapter 8

Robert E. Lee – Part 1

1807-1870

Robert E. Lee at age 31, by William Edward West, 1838

Not all the heroes of the Civil War were in the Northern Army. The South had its great leaders, although it fought a losing fight. The greatest of these was the commander-in-chief of the Confederate Army, General Robert Edward Lee. Two members of his family were signers of the Declaration of Independence. "Light Horse Harry" Lee, the father of Robert, was a general in the Revolutionary War.

During Robert E. Lee's boyhood he heard many tales of army life from his father and the friends who visited the plantation in Westmoreland County. When he was eighteen he decided to become a soldier and was sent to West Point. Officers are trained there for the United States Army. He spent four years there and was known as a good student. When graduation came he was second in his class, and was made a lieutenant in a company of engineers.

His work as an engineer took him all over the country. At Fortress Monroe, Virginia, he strengthened the walls and improved the harbor defenses. He spent a few months in Washington, and then was sent to St. Louis, Missouri. The Mississippi River often overflowed its banks at that point, and Lee was ordered to build walls that would keep the water in its channel. He succeeded in building up the shores by driving huge logs, or piles, along the water-front. When this work was done he was called to New York where he improved the defenses in the harbor. Just as he had done at Fortress Monroe.

When war was declared with Mexico, Lee was ordered to the border as chief engineer. Soon he was promoted to the rank of captain. While laying siege to a Mexican town, Captain Lee offered to get information as to the number of the enemy, their exact location, and the best way to attack them. He learned all he wanted to know and was about to return to camp when he saw a party of Mexicans approaching. He hid behind a clump of bushes. The Mexicans rode past him slowly, so close that he could have reached out and touched them. Instead of hurrying back to camp, Lee followed the Mexicans and learned more about them. When he did return he was able to give his general news that helped him to drive out the enemy in that section.

After the Mexican War, Lee spent three years strengthening the defenses of Baltimore. Then he was appointed superintendent of West Point. While in charge of the school he increased the length of time that had to be spent in becoming an army officer to five years. Hardly had he gotten his plans in working order at West Point when he was made a lieutenant-colonel and ordered to join a regiment of cavalry. He would rather have remained at West Point, but he was too good a soldier to refuse to obey orders or to complain.

Shortly after his transfer to the regiment of cavalry, Lee's regiment was sent to Texas. That state had been admitted recently to the Union and the people were being troubled by the Indians. Lee spent three years there, ruling the redskins with a firm but gentle hand. During his service in Texas he returned home to Virginia for a short visit. At that time he was called upon to command the United States soldiers who were ordered to capture John Brown and his raiders. Brown had led a party of men against the army store-house at Harper's Ferry, Virginia. He wanted to get guns and ammunition with which to begin a war against all slave owners. Brown was surrounded by Lee's troops and forced to surrender. Later Lee returned to Texas.

In 1861 the question of slavery between the North and South reached such a point that the Southern States were threatening to withdraw from the Union. Many men in the North did not want this to happen. There were also many in the South who believed that the nation should not be split in two. When Abraham Lincoln was elected to the presidency the southerners felt that all hope of settling the slavery question was gone. Every one knew of Lincoln's dislike for slavery. The slave owners were sure they would be forced to give up their slaves, so they decided to be the first to act.

Lee knew that war was bound to come between the Northern and Southern States. As an officer in the United States Army he would have to lead his men against his southern friends and relatives. His family was in Virginia and all his sons were slave owners. On the other hand, he felt that the Southern States were wrong in fighting the United States Government and that the result would be a bloody war. It was hard for Robert Lee to decide whether to remain in the army and fight his friends and relatives in the South, or withdraw from the army and fight against the government. In the end he decided that he could not draw his sword against his children, his friends and the people of his native state. Having made this decision, he resigned from the United States Army.

As soon as Lee gave up his position in the United States Army the president of the Confederacy, Jefferson Davis, made him secretary of war. He took full charge of the coast defenses in the South. The harbors were prepared to resist attack. Food, ammunition, and other supplies were gathered in preparation for a long struggle.

In 1862 Lee was made commander-in-chief of the Armies of the South. His men soon learned to love and respect him. At all times he was ready and willing to help them. One day he issued an order which stated that no one was to be given leave of absence. Shortly afterward a private called upon him and said that he would like to have ten days' leave so that he could go home. He had left his wife and child with a few slaves. He had received word that the slaves were running away. He wanted to return in order to get them and put them to work with the Southern Army. In this way he would be sure they would earn enough to support his wife. Lee hardly knew what to say when the soldier had finished speaking. He could not go back on the order which he had just written and he did not want to refuse the request. After much thought he found a way out. He sent an order to the man's captain putting the soldier on secret service duty for ten days. Lee told the man to learn all he could about the Union Army. At the same time he might visit his home.

Lee had great success with his armies during the first year he was in command. He pushed his way north through Maryland and into Pennsylvania. The North was alarmed. First they thought he would attack Washington, but he passed the capital without stopping. No one knew where he was going, and the excitement grew. A Northern Army was sent to stop his march. The two armies met at Gettysburg on the first of July, 1863. The armies gathered on opposite hills and the fight began. Victory at first was on the side of the South, but reinforcements for the North turned the tide of battle. General Lee, on horseback, looked over the field with his glasses, and directed the move-

ments of his troops. Officers hurried back and forth, carrying out his orders. For three days the battle raged and the Confederates prepared for a final struggle to force the Northern Army to withdraw. The finest men of the South were placed under General Pickett and hurled against the Union lines. With fifteen thousand men he marched up the slope which sheltered the northern soldiers. A rifle and artillery fire cut down the southerners like a reaper cuts hay, but their ranks did not break. When the Confederates reached the Union lines they met a wall of bayonets. During the fierce hand-to-hand struggle which followed more lives were lost and many prisoners were captured. Pickett's men were worn out by their dash up the hill, and they could not hold the position which they had won. The few that were left were swept back, and the crushed but still undefeated Confederate Army slowly retreated

Robert E. Lee, by Edward Caledon Bruce, 1865

across the Potomac into Virginia. The war continued for nearly two years before they were finally forced to surrender.

It was not until after the siege of Petersburg and the fall of Richmond that General Lee surrendered to Grant at Appomattox Court House, Virginia, April 9, 1865. Lee agreed that his men would lay down their guns, return to their homes, and no longer fight against the Union. In parting from his men who had fought so nobly for the cause they believed to be right, Lee said, "Men, we have fought through the war together; I have done my best for you; my heart is too full to say more."

After the war General Robert E. Lee returned to his native state, Virginia. He accepted the presidency of Washington College, at Lexington. There were very few students in the South who could afford to go to college after the war, but Lee began to build up the school and make it worthy of George Washington, after whom it was named. For five years he served as president of the school. During that time he did all he could to rejoin the North and South. When he died his old horse, "Traveler," was led, riderless, by two soldiers behind the hearse.

Chapter 9

ஐ

Robert E. Lee – Part 2

1807-1870

One of the bravest and most brilliant officers America has ever produced was General Robert E. Lee. He was a native of Virginia. When the Civil War broke out, although he opposed secession, he believed that his first duty was to Virginia. He chose to fight for his native state rather than for the Union.

Lee lived at Arlington on a beautiful estate just across the Potomac River from Washington. During the war this estate was seized by the Federal Government. Today it is a national soldiers' cemetery. Here repose, in their last sleep, thousands of soldiers who gave their lives for their country.

Lee's father was Light Horse Harry Lee of Revolutionary fame. When the boy Robert was eleven years old his father died. Robert attended school in Arlington, preparing to enter West Point. At eighteen he was a cadet in the National Military Academy.

At West Point he was a model student. All his work was well done. His uniform was spotless and his gun polished till it shone. He was a joy to the officer in charge of inspection.

Robert E. Lee, by John Adams Elder

The young cadet held, successively, the various offices open to the students. At graduation Lee was cadet adjutant, the highest honor attainable. He was graduated second in a class of 46.

After graduation he was appointed second lieutenant in the Engineers' Corps, a position open only to the best students.

40

The engineers' work was along the coast lines and near the cities. This kept the young lieutenant in the life that he liked. He was fond of social life and was as much at home in the drawing room as in the barracks.

Two years after graduation he married Mary Custis. His wife was the daughter of the adopted son of George Washington. Her grandmother was Martha Custis, George Washington's wife.

While in the Engineers' Corps he was busy planning and supervising the strengthening of the coast defences of the country. Later he was sent to the Mississippi to assist in work to compel the waters of that river to stay in its channel. His work has stood the ravages of the river and is still in good working order.

During the Mexican War he served with honor and distinction, receiving the hearty approval of General Winfield Scott, his commanding officer.

In 1852 Lee was appointed Superintendent of West Point. For three years he directed this military college.

Relieved from this duty, he went west, a lieutenant colonel in the cavalry. About this time Mrs. Lee's father died, leaving her his large estate at Arlington. Lee did not like the work in the West. The wild life, the lack of social activities, contact with the Indians, none of these appealed to him.

In 1861 Robert E. Lee reached the decisive point in his life. In April of that year Virginia decided to leave the Union. Just before this General Scott sent Mr. Blair to Lee, offering him the command of the Union Army. Lee replied, "I declined the offer…stating that though opposed to secession and deprecating war, I could take no part in an invasion of the Southern States." A few days later he resigned from the Federal Army, declaring that he would never draw his sword again save in the defense of his native state.

Jefferson Davis was made president of the new government formed by the Southern States. He called Robert E. Lee to command the Southern armies in Virginia.

Most of the battles of the war were fought in Virginia. General Lee was soon in command of all the Southern armies. He led them to many a victory. For four long years his masterly generalship kept the Union forces out of Richmond. He led his armies into Pennsylvania. The people in Philadelphia were filled with dismay. Could the Union forces stop his advance? The two armies met at Gettysburg. For three days the battle raged. On the third day the torn and shattered Confederate forces were compelled to retreat. It was an orderly retreat, General Lee seeing his army safely across the Potomac River.

At the end of the war General Lee was released on his promise not to take up arms again against the Union. His home was gone, money was scarce, but a kind friend offered his family a home in a quiet part of Virginia. He accepted.

When the news of Lincoln's assassination reached him, he denounced it. That kind of warfare had no appeal for him. He knew also that Lincoln was one of the best friends the South could have.

President Johnson said that all the Southerners could apply for pardon. General Lee was one of the first to make application. He felt it was his duty. Said he to a friend, "If you intend to reside in this country, and wish to do your part in the restoration of your state and in the government of the country, which I think is the duty of every citizen to do, I know of no objections to your taking the amnesty oath." From this time on Lee used his influence to bring about peace and good will in the South. He tried to heal the wounds made by the war, and to create conditions that would lead to

At the Front, by George Cochran Lambdin, 1866

good relations between the South and the North.

At this time he was asked to become President of Washington College. This college had been almost destroyed during the war. Lee accepted the trust. Under his wise administration the college recovered rapidly. He was personally interested in each student. Here he had a fine chance to teach them to forget the old sores of the war and to look forward to peaceful relations with their northern friends. He served the college faithfully until his death in 1870.

General Lee was a great man. He fought valiantly in a lost cause, but when the struggle was over, realizing that the cause was lost, he threw himself heart and soul into the work of restoring his state to the Union.

The Heart of Lee

His spirit of moderation toward his foes was illustrated with singular beauty in an incident that occurred at Gettysburg, after the close of the battle. "I was badly wounded," says a private of the Army of the Potomac. "A ball had shattered my left leg. I lay on the ground not far from Cemetery Ridge, and as General Lee ordered his retreat, he and his officers rode near me. As he came along I recognized him, and though faint from exposure and loss of blood, I raised up my hands, looked Lee in the face, and shouted as loud as I could, 'Hurrah for the Union.'

"The general heard me, looked, stopped his horse, dismounted, and came toward me. I confess I at first thought he meant to kill me. But as he came up, he looked down at me with such a sad expression on his face, that all fear left me, and I wondered what he was about. He extended his hand to me and grasping mine firmly and looking right into my eyes, said, 'My son, I hope you will soon be well.'

"If I live a thousand years, I will never forget the expression on General Lee's face. Here we was defeated, retiring from a field that cost him and his cause almost their last hope, and yet he stopped to say words like those to a wounded soldier of the opposition, who had taunted him as he passed by.

"As soon as the general had left me, I cried myself to sleep there upon the bloody ground."

Chapter 10

✌

Ulysses S. Grant – Part 1

1822-1885

Once upon a time, at Point Pleasant, a small town on the Ohio River, there lived a young couple who could not decide how to name their first baby. He was a darling child, and as the weeks went by, and he grew prettier every minute, it was harder and harder to think of a name good enough for him.

Finally Jesse Grant, the father, told his wife, Hannah, he thought it would be a good plan to ask the grandparents' advice. So off they rode from their little cottage, carrying the baby with them.

Lt. Gen. Ulysses S. Grant, by Constant Mayer, 1866

But at grandpa's it was even worse. In that house there were four people besides themselves to suit. At last, the father, mother, grandfather, grandmother, and the two aunts each wrote a favorite name on a bit of paper. These slips of paper were all put into grandpa's tall, silk hat which was placed on the spindle-legged table. "Now," said the father to one of the aunts, "draw from the hat a slip of paper, and whatever name is written on that slip shall be the name of my son."

The slip she drew had the name "Ulysses" on it.

"Well," murmured the grandfather, "our dear child is named for a great soldier of the olden days. But I wanted him to be called Hiram, who was a good king in Bible times."

Then Hannah Grant, who could not bear to have him disappointed, answered: "Let him have

44

both names!" So the baby was christened Hiram Ulysses Grant.

While Ulysses was still a baby, his parents moved to Georgetown, Ohio. There his father built a nice new brick house and managed a big farm besides his regular work of tanning leather. As Ulysses got old enough to help at any kind of work, it was plain he would never be a tanner. He hated the smell of leather. But he was perfectly happy on the farm. He liked best of all to be round the horses, and before he was six years old he rode horseback as well as any man in Georgetown. When he was seven, it was part of his work to drive the span of horses in a heavy team that carried the cord-wood from the wood-lot to the house and shop. He must have been a strong boy, for at the age of eleven he used to hold the plow when his father wanted to break up new land, and it makes the arms and back ache to hold a heavy plow! He was patient with all animals and knew just how to manage them. His father and all the neighbors had Ulysses break their colts.

In the winters Ulysses went to school, but he did not care for it as much as he did for outdoor life and work with his hands. Still he usually had his lessons and was decidedly bright in arithmetic. Because he was not a shirk and always told the truth, his father was in the habit of saying, after the farm chores were done: "Now, Ulysses, you can take the horse and carriage and go where you like. I know I can trust you."

When he was only twelve, his father began sending him seventy or eighty miles away from home, on business errands. These trips would take him two days. Sometimes he went alone, and sometimes he took one of his chums with him. Talking so much with grown men gave him an old manner, and as his judgment was pretty good he was called by merchants a "sharp one." He would have been contented to jaunt about the country, trading and colt-breaking, all his life, but his father decided he ought to have military training and obtained for him an appointment at West Point (the United States' school for training soldiers that was started by George Washington) without Ulysses knowing a thing about it. Now Ulysses did not have the least desire to be a soldier and did not want to go to this school one bit, but he had always obeyed his father, and started on a fifteen days' journey from Ohio without any more talk than the simple statement: "I don't want to go, but if you say so, I suppose I must."

He found, when he reached the school, that his name had been changed. Up to this time his initials had spelled HUG, but the senator who sent young Grant's appointment papers to Washington had forgotten Ulysses' middle name. He wrote his full name as Ulysses Simpson Grant, and as it would make much trouble to have it changed at Congress, Ulysses let it stand that way. So instead of being called H-U-G Grant (as he had been by his mates at home) the West Point boys, to tease him, caught up the new initials and shouted "Uncle Sam" Grant, or "United States" Grant — and sometimes "Useless" Grant.

But the Ohio boy was good-natured and only laughed at them. He was a cool, slow-moving chap, well-behaved, and was never known to say a profane word in his life. At this school there was plenty of chance to prove his skill with horses. Ulysses was never happier than when he started off for the riding-hall with his spurs clanking on the ground and his great cavalry sword dangling by his side. Once, mounted on a big sorrel horse, and before a visiting "Board of Directors," he made the highest jump that had ever been known at West Point. He was as modest as could be about this jump, but the other cadets (as the pupils were called) bragged about it till they were hoarse.

After his graduation, Grant, with his regiment, was sent to the Mexican border. In the battle of

Palo Alto he had his first taste of war. Being truthful, he confessed afterwards that when he heard the booming of the big guns, he was frightened almost to pieces. But he had never been known to shirk, and he not only rode into the powder and smoke that day, but for two years proved so brave and calm in danger that he was promoted several times. But he did not like fighting. He was sure of that.

At the end of the Mexican War, Ulysses married a girl from St. Louis, named Julia Dent, and she went to live, as soldiers' wives do, in whatever military post to which he happened to be sent. First the regiment was sta-

General Grant and Horse, Photograph, 1864

tioned at Lake Ontario, then at Detroit, and then, dear me! it was ordered to California!

There were no railroads in those days. People had to go three thousand miles on horseback or in slow, lumbering wagons. This took months and was both tiresome and dangerous. Every little while there would be a deep river to ford, or some wicked Indians skulking round, or a wild beast threatening. The officers decided to take their regiments to California by water. This would be a hard trip but a safer one.

It was lucky that Mrs. Grant and the babies stayed behind with the grandparents, for besides the weariness of the long journey, there was scarcity of food; a terrible cholera plague broke out, and Ulysses Grant worked night and day. He had to keep his soldiers fed, watch out for the Indians, and nurse the sick people.

Well, after eleven years of army life, Grant decided to resign from the service. He thought war was cruel; he wanted to be with his wife and children; and a soldier got such small pay that he wondered how he was ever going to be able to educate the children. Farming would be better than fighting, he said.

He was welcomed home with great joy.

His wife owned a bit of land, and Grant built a log cabin on it. He planted crops, cut wood, kept horses and cows, and worked from sunrise till dark. But the land was so poor that he named the place Hardscrabble. Even with no money and hard work, the Grants were happy until the climate gave Ulysses a fever; then they left Missouri country life and moved into the city of St. Louis.

In this city Grant tried his hand at selling houses, laying out streets, and working in the custom-house; but something went wrong in every place he got. He had to move into poorer houses, he had to borrow money, and finally he walked the streets trying to find some new kind of work. Nobody would hire him. The men said he was a failure. Friends of the Dent family shook their heads as they whispered: "Poor Julia, she didn't get much of a husband, did she?"

Then he went back to Galena, Illinois, and was a clerk in his brother's store, earning about what any fifteen-year-old boy gets to-day. He worked quietly in the store all day, stayed at home evenings, and was called a very "commonplace man." He was bitterly discouraged, I tell you, that he could not get ahead in the world. And his father's pride was hurt to think that his son who had appeared so smart at twelve could not, as a grown man, take care of his own family. But Julia Dent Grant was sweet and kind. She kept telling him that he would have better luck pretty soon.

In 1861 the Americans began to quarrel among themselves. Several of the States grew very bitter against each other and were so stubborn that the President of the United States, Abraham Lincoln, said he must have seventy-five thousand men to help him stop such rebellion. Ulysses Grant came forward, and said he would be one of these seventy-five thousand, and enlisted again in the United States Army. He was asked to be the colonel of an Illinois regiment by the governor of that State. Then, you may be sure, what he had learned at West Point came into good play. He soon showed that he knew just how to train men into fine soldiers. He did so well that he was made Brigadier-general.

He stormed right through the enemies' lines and took fort after fort. Oh, his work was splendid — this man who had been called a failure!

A general who was fighting against him began to get frightened, and by and by he sent Grant a note saying: "What terms will you make with us if we will give in just a little and do partly as you

Grant and His Generals, by Ole Peter Hansen Balling, 1865

The Union Scout, by Johannes Adam Simon Oertel, 1866

want us to?"

Grant laughed when he read the letter and wrote back: "No terms at all but unconditional surrender!" Finally the other general did surrender, and when the story of the two letters and the victory for Grant was told, the initials of his name were twisted into another phrase; he was called Unconditional Surrender Grant. This saying was quoted for months, every time his name was mentioned. At the end of that time, he had said something else that pleased the people and the President.

You see, the war kept raging harder and harder. It seemed as if it would never end. Grant was always at the front of his troops, watching everything the enemy did and planned, but he grew sadder and sadder. He felt sure there would be fighting until dear, brave Robert E. Lee, the southern general, laid down his sword. The whole country was sad and anxious. They said: "It is time there was a change — what in the world is Grant going to do?" And he answered: "I am going to fight it out on this line if it takes all summer!" No one doubted he would keep his word. It did take all summer and all winter, too. Then, when poor General Lee saw that his men were completely trapped, and that they would starve if he did not give in, he yielded. Grant showed how much of a gentleman he was by his treatment of the general and soldiers he had conquered. There was no lack of courtesy toward them, I can tell you. When the cruel war was ended, Grant was the nation's hero.

Later, Grant was made President of the United States he had saved. When he had finished his term of four years, he was chosen for President again. After that he traveled round the world. I cannot begin to tell you the number of presents he received or describe one half the honors which were paid him — paid to this man who, at one time, could not get a day's work in St. Louis. This farmer from Hardscrabble dined with kings and queens, talked with the Pope of Rome, called on the Czar of Russia, visited the Mikado of Japan in his royal palace, and was given four beautiful homes of his own by rich Americans. One house was in Galena, one in Philadelphia, one in Washington, and another in New York. New York was his favorite city, and in a square named for him you can see a statue showing General Grant on his pet horse, in army uniform. On Claremont Heights where it can be seen from the city, the harbor, and the Hudson River, stands a magnificent tomb, the resting-place of the great hero who was born in the tiny house at Point Pleasant.

There was always a good deal of fighting blood in the Grants. The sixth or seventh great-grandfather of Ulysses, Matthew Grant, came to Massachusetts in 1630, almost three hundred years ago; over in Scotland, where he was born, he belonged to the clan whose motto was "Stand Fast." I think that old Scotchman and all the other ancestors would agree with us that the boy from Ohio stood fast. And how well the name suited him which his aunt drew from the old silk hat — Ulysses — a brave soldier of the olden time!

Grant Accepting Lee's Surrender at Appomattox Court House

Chapter 11

ॐ

Ulysses S. Grant – Part 2

Grant's Last Battle
1822-1885

Although vacations are welcome and rest or change is delightful, there are but few men who like to have nothing to do.

General Grant was not one of these. He liked to be occupied. His trip around the world was over, he was no longer in office or in the army, he was worth just about a hundred thousand dollars. If he could use this money wisely, he thought, he could make a good deal out of it and perhaps be worth a fortune – which would be a good thing for his family.

General Grant and His Family

As you know, the general's tastes were simple. He did love fine horses, he did enjoy a good cigar; but these were his only luxuries.

He was very, very fond of his children. He wished to help them on in the world, and, after his return to America, he was anxious to do something that would occupy his mind and benefit his family.

He had been given many presents by his fellow countrymen. They insisted on showing him how much they thought of what he had done for them and the republic. He was given a fine house in Galena, one in Philadelphia, one in Washington, and one in New York. The men who had money made him a gift of two hundred and fifty thousand dollars, the interest of which – that is, the money it earns each year – was to come to him, while the whole amount was to be kept untouched for his wife and children if he should die.

He had one hundred thousand dollars of his own besides this, and the brownstone house in East Sixty-sixth street, near the Central Park, in New York, was full of presents and trophies and mementoes that had been given him by the princes and people he had visited in his journey around the world.

In 1880 the National Republican Convention met at Chicago to nominate a new president of the United States. Many of the men in that convention wished to nominate General Grant. But there was a strong opposition, not to Grant, but to allowing any man to be president of the United States more than twice.

No president had ever had a third term. Washington had stood out against it when he was asked to serve and his example has always been followed. Probably Grant would not have accepted the nomination, although he never did say anything until it was time to speak.

So the fear that the people would not like it carried the day, and another man was nominated for president. But three hundred and six of the delegates to the convention held firmly together, voting every time for General Grant.

If he had been nominated, and if he had accepted, there is no doubt that he would have been elected, for he was the greatest living American and the people were true to the man who had made almost their very existence possible.

He did not wish the office again; he would not have accepted it or served had he not felt that it was the will of the people. To that he always bowed obedience. It is probable, had he been elected, that he would have made a better president than ever, for his trip around the world had given him a new knowledge of men and of nations, and that experience would have aided him greatly in conducting, the affairs of the republic and keeping it up to the mark alongside the rest of the world.

But, instead of a political campaign, he had another fight before him – the fiercest, most unrelenting and most desperate of any that it had ever fallen to the lot of the great soldier to face and wage.

He was sixty years old; he was healthy, wealthy and wise. The world was going well with him. His fame was at its highest. His name was honored throughout all the world. It seemed as though nothing could disturb or molest him, and yet, at one blow, the old general was struck down – wounded in the tenderest of all places – his honor – his reputation – his word.

It was this way. In 1880 he had gone into business, investing the hundred thousand dollars, of which I have told you, in the banking business in which one of his sons was a partner.

The banking business, you know, is one that deals with money; lending, using or investing it so as to get large returns and good profits. It is a very fine and high-toned business when honorably conducted. But it gives opportunity to a dishonest or bad man to harm and hurt other people, by what is called speculation.

General Grant was not an active partner in the business. He put in all his money and was to have part of the profits. He had perfect confidence in his son and his son's partner.

At first the firm made lots of money. General Grant's name, of course, gave people confidence and one of the partners was such a sharp and shrewd business man that people called him the "Napoleon of finance" – which means that he was such a good hand to manage money matters that he could conquer everything opposed to him in business, just as Napoleon did in war. But Napoleon, you know, was defeated and utterly overthrown at Waterloo!

It was the night before Christmas in the year 1883, when General Grant, as I have told you, was feeling that everything was going finely with him, that he was well and strong and that he was very nearly a millionaire on the profits of his banking business, that he slipped on the ice in front of his house and hurt one of his muscles so badly that he had to go to bed and was kept indoors for weeks. You would not think a little fall like that would be so bad, but when a man gets to be over sixty he does not get over the shock of such an accident as easily as he did when he was sixteen. From that Christmas day of 1883 General Grant was never again a well man.

Still he felt comfortable in his mind, for his affairs were prosperous, and for the first time in his life he was able to buy what he pleased and to spend as he liked, with a good big sum in the bank.

On the morning of Tuesday, the sixth of May, 1884, General Grant was, as he thought, a millionaire. Before sunset that same day he knew that he was ruined.

The bank had failed. The "Napoleon of finance" whom everyone thought so smart a business man, had been too smart. He had speculated and lost everything.

Worse than this, he had lied and stolen. He had used the name and fame of General Grant to back up wicked schemes and dishonorable transactions; he had used up all the money put into the business by General Grant and Mrs. Grant and the others who had gladly put in the money because of General Grant's name, and he had so turned and twisted and handled things that not a dollar was left in the business. General Grant and his sons were ruined; their good names apparently, were disgraced by being mixed up with the affairs and wickednesses of their bad and bold partner, who, as soon as he saw the truth was out ran away, like the thief and coward he was.

Every one was surprised. More than this, they were so startled that, for a time, even the great name of Grant seemed beclouded, and thoughtless people, cruel people, the folks who like to talk and to say things without thinking of the consequences, said mean and hateful and wicked and untruthful things about this great and noble soldier who never in his life had done a dishonorable act, or said a mean or unkind thing, or knowingly injured a single person. It was hard, was it not?

It was especially hard on such a man as General Grant. He never complained, he never spoke of the treatment to his friends; but it hurt terribly.

It made him sick. It weakened a constitution already undermined by the shock of that fall on the ice, and it developed a terrible trouble in his throat that brought him months of suffering, of torture and of agony.

Before this developed however, he had set to work to do something to earn money. For, to make a bad matter worse, something was wrong with the way the trust fund of $250,000, of which I have told you, was invested and no money could come from that for months. A great magazine wished him to tell for its readers the story of one of his battles, and, although General Grant had never tried or even thought of such a thing, he did set to work, and wrote the story of how he fought the battle of Shiloh; then he wrote another one telling how he captured Vicksburg.

It was while he was at work on these articles that the trouble in his throat developed. It grew worse and worse. The doctors could not cure it; they could hardly give him relief from the pain that came; and the first struggle with the dreadful disease was harder to stand than any battle-grip he had ever wrestled with.

At first he was discouraged. For, as he looked at the wreck of his fortune made by the dreadful business failure, and knew that he was a sick man, no longer able to work or make his own living, the future looked very dark and he could not see how he could make things better for his wife or the boys he so dearly loved.

Then it was that he determined to write, as did Julius Caesar, the story of his life, his battles and his campaigns. Publishers in different parts of the country, when they saw how interesting were the two articles he had published and how interested the people were in reading them, knew that his story of the war would be a very successful book and made him all sorts of offers and promises, if he would write it.

He saw a way out of his difficulties; he determined to try. Then the world saw one of the most remarkable things in all its long history – a sick man, without experience or training, deliberately sitting down to write the story of his life, fighting off death with all the might and strength of his giant will, in order to save his name from dishonor and leave something for his wife and children after the death that he knew was not far away.

In his room in the second story of that vine-covered brownstone house in Sixty-sixth street the fight went on. Now up, now down; sometimes so improved that every one, save the doctor, was full of hope; now down so low that the faltering breath nearly stopped, and only by stimulants was life bought back and death held at bay,

Ulysses S. Grant writing his memoirs on the porch of the cottage on Mt. McGregor in 1885

53

thus he lived; and still the pencil kept going busily, whenever there was a pause in the weakness or the pain. Writing or dictating, sometimes four, sometimes six, sometimes eight hours a day, so the months went on, until, at last, on the 9th of June, 1885, he was removed to Mount McGregor near Saratoga, in New York, and there, almost within sight of a famous field of battle and surrender in which his forefathers had joined, the fight for life and for strength to finish his work went on.

It was a tremendous effort. He had barely two months to live; but, in the eight weeks that followed the first of May, he did more work, in writing his book, than in any other eight weeks of his life. As an army in battle sometimes gathers up all its strength for a final charge or for a last stand against the foe, so the old general, weakened by disease, worried by anxiety, but determined to win, actually held death at bay until the work he had set himself to do was accomplished.

Think of it, boys and girls, for it is one of the most remarkable things that ever happened, the most heroic act in all this great soldier's wonderful career.

And the book that he wrote and completed under those fearful conditions is one of the world's notable books, while its success more than met the desires of the writer and placed his family again in comfort and security.

It was a wonderful victory.

As he lay there sick, dying, but working manfully and well, the sympathy of all the world went out to him. Friend and foe, Northerner and Southerner, American and alien, prince and king, workingman and laborer, the high and the humble, men and women, old and young – from all these, all over the land and across the seas in the countries he had visited, came words of sympathy, of inquiry and of affection which showed how all the world loves and honors and reveres a real hero.

From his sick room went out this message to the world, whispered with stammering tones.

"I am very much touched and grateful for the sympathy and interest manifested in me by my friends and by those who have not hitherto been regarded as my friends. I desire the good-will of all, whether heretofore friends or not."

At last, the work was done. The book was finished. On the first day of July, 1885, his preface was dated and signed. On the next day, silently thinking over what he had done, what he had suffered and what might still be before him, he wrote a remarkable letter to his doctors which closed in this way: "If it is within God's providence," he wrote, "that I should go now, I am ready to obey his call without a murmur – I should prefer going now to enduring my present suffering for a single day without hope of recovery. As I have stated, I am thankful for the Providential extension of my time to enable me to continue my work. I am further thankful, and in a much greater degree thankful, because it has enabled me to see for myself the happy harmony which so suddenly sprung up between those engaged but a few years ago in deadly conflict. It has been an inestimable blessing to me to hear the kind expressions toward me in person from all parts of the country, from people of all nationalities, of all religions and of no religion, of Confederates and National troops alike. They have brought joy to my heart, if they have not affected a cure. So to you and your colleagues I acknowledge my indebtedness for having brought me through the valley of the shadow of death to enable me to witness these things."

You see, to the last, the great soldier's thoughts were all for peace. He had seen battles. He knew the horrors of war. He knew the beauty of peace.

With his work finished, his desire for life was gone. He knew what life meant – suffering. He wished release and peace. A few days longer he lingered on, then, quietly, calmly, in the cottage on the mountain top came the end. The last fight was over; the last victory had been won.

On the morning of the twenty-third of July, 1885, the tired hand dropped limply within that of the patient, faithful wife. Then the telegraph clicked; a brief message went abroad over all the earth; the flag on the White House at Washington dropped to half-mast. General Grant was dead.

Chapter 12

Thomas "Stonewall" Jackson

1824-1863

General Thomas J. ("Stonewall") Jackson,
from *Abraham Lincoln* by John G. Nicolay and John Hay, 1890

Next to General Lee, the man who did most for the Southern cause was General Jackson. You will be interested to know how he won his curious nickname of "Stonewall."

It was at the first battle of Bull Run, or Manassas. The Confederate left had retreated a mile or more. The Carolina and Georgia troops were in great confusion. The commanders were vainly trying to rally them. Those in retreat at length "reached the plateau where Jackson and his brigade were stationed. The brigade never wavered, but stood fast and held the position."

"See there!" shouted General Bee, "Jackson is standing like a stone wall. Rally on the Virginians!"

Rally they did, and Jackson was thereafter known as "Stonewall."

The name of Stonewall passed over to the brigade commanded by General Jackson. How proud he was of his men! Once he had left them for a while to find them, on his return, in battle and retreating. Instantly he placed himself at their head with the words, "The 'Stonewall Brigade' never retreats. Follow me back to the field!"

Jackson was stern in discipline. This was because he was so intensely in earnest. Once, when an early start was to be made, he ordered breakfast to be served to his staff officers at seven. Prompt to the hour appeared Jackson. The simple meal was ready, but where were the officers? "Pour the coffee into the road!" ordered Jackson. It was done, and, in this way, a very effective lesson in promptness was taught.

His men would have followed Jackson blindfold. "Jackson threw them into battle like the guns behind the galloping horses. He made them accomplish tasks amid the firing in which they grew twice their stature as soldiers, and then he gave them rest. When they saw…the odd grim figure of the being who bent them to these feats, they loved that man. 'Old Stonewall' filled the soldier's eye like a battle flag. The sight of him brought out tears."

Jackson was an earnest Christian. Every morning he read his Bible and then prayed. He never made a raid, or entered into battle without asking divine guidance and help. In the heat of the conflict he often prayed. Thousands saw his right arm and even both arms raised to heaven. Those nearer saw his lips move. "Like Joshua of old, he prayed with up-lifted hand for victory."

After the second battle of Bull Run, or Manassas, Jackson and an army surgeon were sitting by the fire drinking coffee out of their tin cups. "We have won this battle by the hardest kind of fighting," said the surgeon. But Jackson's reply was "No, no; we have won it by the blessing of Almighty God."

Battle of Chancellorsville

Stonewall Jackson's victories had won him great renown. Everybody was anxious to see him, but he was so retiring in his habits that he shunned the public gaze. His dress was generally so shabby that many did not know him, even when they saw him on his old sorrel horse. Once he was riding with some of his officers through a field of oats. The owner ran after them in a rage, demanding Jackson's name, that he might report him at headquarters.

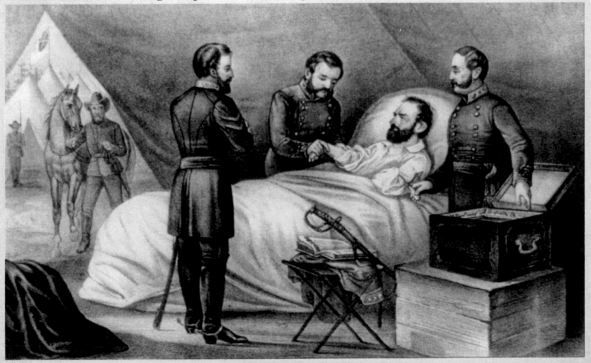

Death of Stonewall Jackson

57

"Jackson is my name, sir," replied the general.

"What Jackson?" inquired the farmer.

"General Jackson."

"What! Stonewall Jackson!" exclaimed the man in astonishment.

"That is what they call me," replied Jackson.

"General," said the man, taking off his hat, "ride over my whole field. Do whatever you like with it, sir."

The death of Jackson was most tragic. Through a mistake, he was shot by his own men at Chancellorsville. With a few officers, he had gone to reconnoiter the Federal position. On his return the little party were taken for the foe, and a whole regiment blazed out upon them. Jackson, severely wounded, was carried to the rear. It was hoped that he might recover, but he died after eight days with these beautiful words upon his lips, "Let us pass over the river and rest under the shade of the trees."

Confederate Soldiers Monument, Hawkinsville, Pulaski County, Georgia

Chapter 13

❧

A Teamster at Gettysburg

July 1863

The steamer from Newbern, that carried the wagon-train of which Jim Wright had charge, proceeded directly to Baltimore. At this place all of the officers' baggage and the camp equipage of the 76th Regiment were dumped out. The wagons were then reloaded with ammunition, and rushed to the front.

It was late in the afternoon of July 2d when Jim's wagons reached the vicinity of Gettysburg. All day they had heard the sound of cannon, and toward noon had met streams of wounded and squads of prisoners under guard.

Now the officers were continually hurrying the trains forward, and as Jim's teams were in excellent condition, his train was in advance of the others. He could hear musketry rattling furiously over beyond the hills on the left, when a staff officer came galloping up to the wagons.

"What have you in those wagons?"

"Ammunition, sir; E. B. cartridges, caliber .58," answered Jim, promptly.

"Good! Get those wagons up to the front as quickly as possible! Kill your teams if necessary, but get there! The left of our line is being flanked, and the men are nearly out of ammunition. Hurry, for God's sake, hurry!"

"Show me where to go, captain, and I'll shove those wagons there as quick as mules can take them," answered Jim.

"Come on!" The officer dashed ahead. "I'll show you."

The captain led Jim's train from the main road, up a slight elevation, and then, looking down the steep hill and out into the field beyond, Jim saw the Union line. Flashes and puffs of smoke beyond that marked the enemy's position.

A division of regulars was retiring slowly; on their left one battered brigade was stretched out in single rank, with their left flank "refused," or bent back like a door on a hinge.

"O Lord, we are too late! The enemy are on our road!" shouted the officer, in dismay.

"Captain," said Jim, scanning the ground, "I can take a wagon down that hill, across that wheatfield, swing to the left, and give those boys ammunition."

"If you could you might save the whole army. But can you?" the captain cried.

The feat looked impossible. The hill seemed too steep. The likelihood that the wagon would overrun the team and be upset, and the whole load lost, was very great. Once at the bottom, however, the teamster would be all right.

"I can tie a couple of dead mules to the hind end of the wagon, and they will act as brakes. I've let wagons down gulches worse than this," said Jim, confidently.

59

Battle of Gettysburg, by Peter Frederick Rothermel, 1870

"But where are your dead mules?"

"Here, captain," and Jim pointed to the leaders of a team. "I'll tie them on behind the wagon, and," touching his pistol, "when we begin to go down the hill they'll be dead!"

"Good! good!" said the captain. "Go ahead; it's our only chance. But be quick!"

"Sam," said Jim, addressing the black driver, "I want you to drive your team down there."

"Yes, boss, I hear yo'," was the stolid answer.

"I'm going along with you, Sam," said Jim. "It's mighty hot down there; we may both be killed; but those cartridges have got to go to the boys in that line — understand?"

"Sergeant Jim," said Sam, "did de cap'n say dat dis load ob ca'tridges mout sabe de army?"

"That's what he said, Sam."

"Den, boss, I's a-gwine ter take dem ca'tridges dere. Jes' yo' show de way. I's a-gwine ter stay wid yo'!"

"Bully boy, Sam! That's the kind of talk! We aren't killed yet, and I hope we won't be."

Then Jim, having pointed out the course he wished the negro to take, tied the two mules doomed to serve as brakes to the rear of the wagon, and stripped off the canvas cover.

"Come on!" yelled the officer.

Sam leaped into the saddle, cracked his whip, and shouted, "Git — yo'!" and the wagon started.

It was but a short distance to the summit; then came a steep, rough descent to the rolling field where the Union line was fighting. As they reached the crest, Jim's revolver cracked twice, and the two mules fell. Away the wagon went, plunging, crashing down the hill, and would have been dashed to pieces had it not been steadied, and its speed checked by Jim's ingenious brake. At the base of the hill his keen knife severed the halters of the dead mules without slackening the speed of the team, and the wagon went flying toward the blue line.

The hissing, humming bullets were everywhere; splinters flew from the wagon, and with a shriek Jim's horse stumbled and went down.

Jim sprang from the saddle and ran beside the team, shouting at the mules, and soon the wagon was in the rear of the forefront of battle.

Back from the firing line the sergeants came running and eagerly seized the pine boxes of cartridges. A mule went down; his harness was quickly cut and the wagon rolled on. The captain's horse was shot under him; he fell with it and Jim and Sam saw him no more.

At the next halt, soldiers with powder-blackened lips, bloodshot eyes and ashen faces were round them, yelling, "Cartridges! cartridges! cartridges!" and more of the pine boxes were quickly pitched out and smashed, and the cartridges in each distributed to the men.

"Pass the word for the boys to hold on hard a little longer — the Sixth Corps is coming on the double-quick, and is almost here!" shouted Jim, as he gave out the ammunition.

"They'll have to come mighty soon, or they'll be too late," said a sergeant. The leading mules had been shot. Only three remained; but on went the wagon, Sam holding the leader by the head.

But a slight hollow seemed to afford some protection, and Jim led Sam that way. They were almost there when a withering volley felled one of the remaining beasts. Instantly Jim's knife cut

The First Day at Gettysburg, by James Alexander Walker

the beast out; then Sam grasped the yoke on the wagon-pole, exerting all his strength, and yelling at the remaining mule, while Jim pushed behind, and all together, with one desperate, final effort, they rolled the wagon into the little hollow! At that instant a bursting shell crashed over their heads, scattering its fragments in every direction, and the faithful negro and the last mule went down together.

The soldiers came running for the few remaining cartridges, and Jim Wright, picking up a musket which one of the wounded men had dropped, ran with them to the line.

"Stay with them, boys! stay with them!" he yelled. "The old Sixth Corps is almost here! Hurrah! hurrah! hurrah! there they come! There's the white cross, boys!"

Down the side of Little Round Top, in magnificent order, two full brigades came pouring on the run. Then the feeble cheer that went up from the hard-pressed line was drowned in the crashing volley that came from the troops of the Sixth Corps, whose advance struck the enemy's right flank, threw the men into disorder, and quickly drove them back into the shelter of the thick woods beyond the field.

The rays of the setting sun were touching the crest of Round Top when the firing ceased, and Jim Wright made his way back to the wagon. There the black man still lay, face downward, beside the dead mule, and a froth was on his lips. Jim snatched from the wagon-box a canteen in which remained a pint or more of precious water, knelt beside his driver, raised his head, and poured a little water between his lips. The drops revived the wounded man; he opened his eyes, and a smile came over his face. "De ca'tridges done got yere in time?" "Yes, Sam, they got here just in time." "Den, boss, it's all right. Tell de boys dat ole Sam — done stay by — as long as he las'."

"He was black and a hero. He gave his life for his country as truly as any soldier," said Jim to a grizzled sergeant.

Chapter 14

❧

Little Eddie the Drummer Boy

A few days before our regiment received orders to join General Lyon, on his march to Wilson's Creek, the drummer of our company was taken sick and conveyed to the hospital. On the night before the march, a negro was arrested within the lines of the camp, and brought before our captain, who asked him what business he had within the lines. He replied: "I know a drummer that you would like to enlist in your company, and I have come to tell you of it." He was immediately requested to inform the drummer that if he would enlist for our short term of service, he would be allowed extra pay, and to do this he must be on the ground early in the morning.

On the following morning there appeared before the captain's quarters during the beating of the reveille, a middle-aged woman, dressed in deep mourning, leading by the hand a sharp, sprightly-looking boy, apparently about twelve or thirteen years of age. Her story was soon told. She was from East Tennessee, where her husband had been killed by the Confederates and all their property destroyed.

During the rehearsal of her story the little fellow kept his eyes intently fixed upon the countenance of the captain, who was about to express a determination not to take so small a boy, when he spoke out: "Don't be afraid, captain, I can drum." This was spoken with so much confidence that the captain immediately observed, with a smile: "Well, well, sergeant, bring the drum, and order our fifer to come forward." In a few moments the drum was produced, and our fifer, a tall, good-natured fellow, who stood, when erect, something over six feet in height, soon made his appearance.

Upon being introduced to his new comrade, he stooped down, with his hands resting upon his knees, and, after peering into the little fellow's face a moment, he observed: "My little man, can you drum?" — "Yes, sir," he replied, "I drummed in Tennessee." Our fifer immediately commenced straightening himself upward until all the angles in his person had disappeared, when he placed his fife at his mouth and played the "Flowers of Edinborough," one of the most difficult things to follow with the drum that could have been selected, and nobly did the little fellow follow him, showing himself to be a master of the drum. When the music ceased, our captain turned to the mother, and observed, "Madam, I will take your boy. What is his name?"

"Edward Lee," she replied; then, placing her hand upon the captain's arm, she continued, "Captain, if he is not killed" — here her maternal feelings overcame her utterance, and she bent down over her boy and kissed him upon the forehead. As she rose, she observed: "Captain, you will bring him back with you, won't you? "

"Yes, yes," he replied, "we will be certain to bring him back with us. We shall be discharged in six weeks."

An hour after, our company led the Iowa First out of camp, our drum and fife playing "The girl

63

I left behind me." Eddie, as we called him, soon became a great favorite with all the men in the company. When any of the boys had returned from a foraging excursion, Eddie's share of the peaches and melons was the first apportioned out. During our heavy and fatiguing march, it was often amusing to see our long-legged fifer wading through the mud with our little drummer mounted upon his back, and always in that position when fording streams.

During the fight at Wilson's Creek, I was stationed with a part of our company on the right of Totten's battery, while the balance of our company, with a part of an Illinois regiment, was ordered

The Death of General Sedgwick, by Julian Scott, 1887

down into a deep ravine upon our left, in which it was known a portion of the enemy was concealed, with whom they were soon engaged. The contest in the ravine continuing some time, Totten suddenly wheeled his battery upon the enemy in that quarter, when they soon retreated to the high ground behind their lines. In less than twenty minutes after Totten had driven the enemy from the ravine, the word passed from man to man throughout the army, "Lyon is killed!" and soon after, hostilities having ceased upon both sides, the order came for our main force to fall back upon Springfield, while a part of the Iowa First and two companies of the Missouri regiment were to camp upon the ground and cover the retreat next morning. That night I was detailed for guard duty, my turn of guard closing with the morning call. When I went out with the officer as a relief, I found that my post was upon a high eminence that overlooked the deep ravine in which our men had engaged the enemy, until Totten's battery came to their assistance. It was a dreary, lonesome beat. The moon had gone down in the early part of the night, while the stars twinkled dimly through a hazy atmosphere, lighting up imperfectly the surrounding objects. The hours passed slowly away, when at length the morning light began to streak along the eastern sky, making surrounding objects more plainly visible. Presently I heard a drum beat up the morning call. At first I thought it came from the camp of the enemy across the creek; but as I listened, I found that it came up from the deep ravine; for a few minutes it was silent, and then I heard it again. I listened — the sound of the drum was familiar to me — and I knew that it was our drummer boy from Tennessee.

I was about to desert my post to go to his assistance, when I discovered the officer of the guard approaching with two men. We all listened to the sound, and were satisfied that it was Eddie's drum. I asked permission to go to his assistance. The officer hesitated, saying that the orders were to march in twenty minutes. I promised to be back in that time, and he consented. I immediately started down the hill through the thick undergrowth, and upon reaching the valley I followed the sound of the drum, and soon found him, seated upon the ground, his back leaning against the trunk of a fallen tree, while his drum hung upon a bush in front of him, reaching nearly to the ground. As soon as he discovered me he dropped his drumsticks and exclaimed, "O corporal! I am so glad to see you. Give me a drink, please," reaching out his hand for my canteen, which was empty. I immediately turned to bring him some water from the brook that I could hear rippling through the bushes near by, when, thinking that I was about to leave him, he began crying, saying: "Don't leave me, corporal — I can't walk." I was soon back with the water, when I discovered that he was seriously wounded in both of his feet by a cannonball. After satisfying his thirst, he looked up into my face and said: "You don't think I will die, corporal, do you? This man said I would not — he said the surgeon could cure my feet." I now discovered a man lying on the grass near him. By his dress I recognized him as belonging to the enemy. It appeared

Wounded Drummer Boy, by Eastman Johnson

that he had been shot through the bowels, and fallen near where Eddie lay. Knowing that he could not live, and seeing the condition of the boy, he had crawled to him, taken off his buckskin suspenders, and corded the little fellow's legs below the knee, and then lay down and died. While he was telling me these particulars, I heard the tramp of cavalry coming down the ravine, and in a moment a scout of the enemy was upon us, and I was taken prisoner. I requested the officer to take Eddie up in front of him, and he did so, carrying him with great tenderness and care. When we reached the camp of the enemy, the little fellow was dead.

✌

Chapter 15

Samuel and Julia Ward Howe

1801-1876
1819-1910

Samuel G. Howe in Dress of a Greek Soldier,
from a drawing by John Elliott

For nearly four hundred years Greece had been subject to Turkey. The Greeks were oppressed and enslaved by their cruel conquerors; they scarcely dared to call their lives their own. At length, in 1821, they resolved to endure oppression no longer. Hopeless as their cause seemed to be, they took up arms and began a war for independence. The Turks were strong and pitiless; the Greeks were poor and weak, and yet they fought bravely for their country and their homes.

The war had been going on for two or three years, when a stranger appeared in Greece who at once attracted much attention. He was a young man of twenty-three or twenty-four. He was very tall and handsome. His long hair was black, his blue eyes were very large, his face was beaming with kindliness and courage.

It was soon learned that this stranger was a young American surgeon and that his name was Samuel G. Howe. He had come to Greece to give such assistance as he could to those who were fighting for liberty.

He began work at once, trying to establish hospitals for the wounded and the sick. He went from one battlefield to another, doing all in his power to relieve the suffering and dying soldiers. Then, when matters seemed to be most desperate, he shouldered a musket and went forth to share with the patriot Greeks the dangers and hardships of war.

He soon learned, however, that a stronger foe than the Turks was threatening the Greeks. That foe was hunger. The war had required so many men that there was now no one left to till the fields. The vineyards had been neglected and trampled down. The cattle had been driven off and butchered. Unless help came, the Greeks would be conquered by starvation.

The young surgeon was not a man to hesitate. He hurried back to America. In letters to the newspapers, in public speeches and personal appeals, he made known the sad condition of the Greeks. Thousands of Americans came forward with gifts of money and food and clothing. A ship was loaded with these generous offerings, and Dr. Howe sailed with it for Greece.

How the poor people of that unfortunate land blessed the stranger who brought this much-needed relief! He gave the food to the famishing, he placed the money in the hands of those who would use it the most wisely for the good of all. The whole nation thanked him.

For a long time after the Greeks had won their independence they remembered with love the brave, handsome American who had done so much to aid them. One story, in particular, they liked to tell and tell again. It was of a Greek

Dr. Samuel Gridley Howe, photograph by Whipple

soldier, whose life the American had saved on the battlefield, and who always afterward followed him about like an affectionate dog. The poet, John Greenleaf Whittier, who knew and loved Dr. Howe, has repeated this story in verse, in which he also briefly alludes to the hero's later services in behalf of humanity.

Julia Ward Howe

Julia Ward was born in New York City, and lived most of her life there and in Boston. Her father was a wealthy banker, with a fine sense of American noblesse oblige. Her mother, a woman of scholarly tastes, died when Julia was only five.

Mr. Ward gave his children every possible advantage; lessons in French and Italian and music, as well as the best English education; and the three daughters had as good a training as the three sons. Julia was an unusual child with a wonderful memory, and learned very quickly. She wrote poems, solemn poems, when a very little girl. At nine she listened at school to recitations in Italian and handed the amazed instructor a composition in that language asking to be allowed to join the class and this request was granted, though the other pupils were twice her age. Life was a serious thing to this child who was brought up very strictly, with duty and dignity constantly impressed

Julia Ward Howe

upon her. She heard frequently stories of her ancestors colonial governors, Revolutionary officers, Nathaniel Greene, and Marion, the "swamp fox of Carolina," the long line passed before the grave little girl, terrible as an army with banners; but always with the trumpet call of inspiration in the thought that they belonged to her.

When she was sixteen her brother returned from several years of study in Germany, and a new world was opened to her German philosophy and poetry, and simultaneously New York society; for at once he made the Ward home one of the social centers of the city. Julia became the reigning favorite and won everybody by her beauty and charm, her tact and ready wit and good humor. She continued her studies regularly, translating German and French and Italian poems, reading philosophy and writing verses.

Visiting in Boston, she made the acquaintance of the literary group there Longfellow, Emerson, Whittier and Holmes. Charles Sumner was her brother's intimate friend, and one day when he and Longfellow were calling on Miss Ward they suggested driving over to the Perkins Institute for the Blind.

They had frequently talked to her of its founder, Doctor Samuel Gridley Howe, the truest hero that America and their century had produced, and withal the best of comrades. The Chevalier, they named him, a Bayard without fear and without reproach. She knew something of the six years he had spent in Greece, fighting during the war for independence and serving as surgeon-in-chief. She knew of his pioneer work for educating the blind, and of his marvelous achievement in teaching Laura Bridgeman the little blind and deaf and dumb girl, the statue which he had brought to life.

When the three friends arrived Doctor Howe was absent, but before they had finished their tour of the building Stunner spied him from the window and called out, "There he is now, on his black horse." The young lady saw him, "a noble rider on a noble steed," and into her life he rode that day, like a medieval chevalier, in spite of the fact that he was forty and she only twenty-four, in spite of the fact that she had lived a gay social

Dr. Samuel G. Howe Teaching Laura Bridgman

life and he was a serious reformer and philanthropist who believed that with the world so full of needy people no one had a right to luxury.

Life with a reformer husband was not always the care-free thing Julia Ward had known, but she had shipped as mate for the voyage, she once said with a merry laugh, and added, "I cannot imagine a more useful motto for married life." She realized always that the deepest and most steadfast part of herself she owed to Doctor Howe. "But for the Chevalier, I should have been merely a woman of the world and a literary dabbler."

With all the cares and joys of a rich home life with her six children, she found time for study and writing. She published two volumes of verse, the first anonymously, but the secret could not be kept, for people declared that no one but Julia Ward Howe could be its author.

In addition to his work for the blind, Doctor Howe edited an anti-slavery paper called the *Boston Commonwealth*, and his wife helped him with that task. Garrison, Sumner, Phillips, Higginson and Theodore Parker became their friends and co-workers. To balance the reformers, Edwin Booth, Holmes, Longfellow and Emerson were frequent guests, drawn by the magnet of Mrs. Howe's personality.

The slavery question became more and more acute, and soon the country was plunged into civil war. Every earnest woman longed to be of some immediate service to the nation and to humanity. Mrs. Howe was fired with the desire to help. Her husband was beyond the age for military duty, her oldest son was a lad, the youngest child two years old. She could not leave home as a nurse. She lacked the practical deftness to prepare lint and hos-

Julia Ward Howe, by John Elliott, c. 1925

pital stores. She seemed to have nothing to give, there was nothing for her to do.

If only her gift for verses were not so slight! If she could but voice the spirit of the hour!

During the autumn of 1861 Julia Ward Howe visited Washington. With friends she went to watch a review of the northern troops, at some distance from the city. While the maneuvers were going on, a sudden movement of the Confederates brought the pageant to a close. Detachments of soldiers galloped to the assistance of a small body of men in danger of being surrounded and cut off from retreat; while the troops remaining were ordered back to camp.

The carriage with the Boston visitors returned very slowly to Washington, for soldiers filled the roads. There were tedious waits while the marching regiments passed them. To beguile the time and to relieve the tense situation, they sang snatches of popular army songs, and one of these was John Brown's Body.

"Good for you!" called out the passing boys in blue, and joined in the chorus with a will, "His soul goes marching on."

"Mrs. Howe," asked James Freeman Clarke, who was in the carriage with her, "why don't you write some really worthy words for that stirring tune?"

"I have often wished to do it," she replied.

And that night her wish was fulfilled. Very early, in the gray of the morning twilight, she awoke and as she waited for the dawn the poem came to her, line by line, till the first stanza was finished. Phrase by phrase, and another stanza! The words came sweeping over her with the rhythm of marching feet. Resistlessly the long lines swung into place before her eyes. "Let us die to make men free, while God is marching on," and the *Battle Hymn of the Republic* was achieved.

"I must get up and write it down, lest I fall asleep again and forget it," she said to herself. In the half light she groped for pen and paper and scrawled the lines down, almost without looking, a thing she had often done before, when verses came to her in the night. With the words put down in black and white, safe from oblivion, she went to sleep again, saying drowsily to herself, "I like this better than most things I have written."

The poem was published soon after in the *Atlantic Monthly,* but aroused little comment. The war, with alternate victory and defeat, engrossed public attention. Small heed could be paid to a few lines in a magazine.

But an army chaplain in Ohio read it, liked it, and memorized it before putting down the *Atlantic.* Captured at Winchester, where he had delayed to help the doctors with the wounded, this chaplain was sent to Libby Prison, in Richmond. One large, comfortless room the Union men had, with the floor for a bed. The Confederate officer in charge told them one night that the South had just had a great victory; and while they sat there in sorrow old Ben, a negro who sold them papers, whispered to one prisoner that this news was false, that Gettysburg had been a great defeat for the South.

The word passed like a flame. Men leaped to their feet, and broke into rejoicings. They shouted and embraced one another in a frenzy of joy and triumph. And the fighting Chaplain McCabe, standing in the middle of that great room, lifted up his fine baritone voice and sang, "Mine eyes have seen the glory of the coming of the Lord." Every voice took up the chorus and "Glory, glory hallelujah, our God is marching on," rang through Lobby Prison. You can imagine the effect of the tremendous uplift of the lines.

Released, the fighting chaplain began work for the Christian Commission and gave a lecture in the hall of representatives in Washington. As part of his recent experiences he told this incident of their celebration of the battle of Gettysburg, and ended by singing Mrs. Howe's poem, as only the man who had lived it could sing it. The great audience was electrified. Men and women sprang to their feet and wept and shouted. Above the wild applause they heard the voice of Abraham Lincoln calling, while the tears rolled down his cheeks, "Sing it again!"

McCabe sang it and the nation took up the chorus. The story of this lecture made the hymn popular everywhere. It was sung in all the homes of the North, at recruiting meetings and rallies. The troops sang it in bivouac at night, and on the march. The Union army seized on it as its battle cry and sang it as they went into action.

This song, which wrote itself in a wonderful moment of inspiration, embodied the very soul of the Union cause. Yet throughout its twenty lines there is no hint of sectional feeling. It was like an electric shock to the people of the North, the call of a silver trumpet, the flash of a lifted sword. It inspired them with hope and courage, giving a new faith in the justice of God. The strength it brought to millions of men and women can never be measured.

And in the world war of the twentieth century, somewhere in France, it was sung over and over. Phrase by phrase, the words fitting new conditions, as they fitted those of the sixties the lightning of His terrible sword, the fiery gospel written in burnished rows of steel, the trumpet that shall never call retreat, sifting out men's hearts before His judgment seat, let us die to make men free—these apply in any warfare or crusade where men are fighting not for self, but for ideals.

After the war was ended Mrs. Howe continued to study, to write essays and poems, to give lectures, to serve in many great causes. But she is best remembered for the message which seemed to come to America, through her loving and sorrowing heart, from God himself, in the *Battle Hymn of the Republic*.

Julia Ward Howe, platinum print, 1908

&

Chapter 16

A Pen Picture of Abraham Lincoln

The most marked characteristic of President Lincoln's manners was his simplicity and artlessness.

This at once impressed itself upon the observation of those who met him for the first time, and each successive interview deepened the impression. People delighted to find in the ruler of the nation freedom from pomposity and affecttation, mingled with a certain simple dignity which never forsook him, even in the presence of critical or polished strangers. There was always something which spoke the fine fibre of the man. While his disregard of courtly conventionalities was something ludicrous, his native sweetness and straightforwardness of manner served to disarm criticism and impress the visitor that he was before a man, pure, self-poised, collected, and strong in unconscious strength.

Portrait of Abraham Lincoln, by George Peter Alexander Healy

The simple habits of Mr. Lincoln were so well known that it is a wonder that he did not sooner lose that precious life which he seemed to hold so lightly. He had an almost morbid dislike for an escort, or guard, and daily exposed himself to the deadly aim of an assassin. "If they kill me," he once said, "the next man will be just as bad for them; and in a country like this, where our habits are simple, and must be, assassination is always possible, and will come if they are determined upon it." A cavalry guard was once placed at the gates

73

of the White House for a while, and he said, privately, that he "worried until he got rid of it."

Gentleness mixed with firmness characterized all of Mr. Lincoln's dealings with public men. Often bitterly assailed and abused, he never appeared to recognize the fact that he had political enemies. His keenest critics and most bitter opponents studiously avoided his presence. It seemed as if no man could be familiar with his homely, heart-lighted features, his single-hearted directness and manly kindliness, and remain long an enemy, or be anything but his friend. It was this warm frankness of Mr. Lincoln's manner that made a hard-headed politician once leave the hustings where Lincoln was speaking in 1856, saying, "I won't hear him, for I don't like a man that makes me believe in him in spite of myself."

"Honest old Abe" has passed into the language of our time and country as a synonym for all that is just and honest in man. Yet thousands of instances, unknown to the world, might be added to those already told of Lincoln's great and crowning virtue. This honesty appeared to spring from religious convictions. This was his surest refuge at times when he was most misunderstood or misrepresented. There was something touching in his childlike and simple reliance upon Divine aid, especially when in such extremities as he sometimes fell into. Though prayer and reading of the Scriptures were his constant habit, he more earnestly than ever, at such times, sought that strength which is promised when mortal help faileth. His address upon the occasion of his re-inauguration has been said to be as truly a religious document as a state-paper; and his acknowledgment of God and His providence are interwoven through all of his later speeches, letters, and messages. Once he said: "I have been driven many times upon my knees by the overwhelming conviction that I had nowhere else to go. My own wisdom and that of all about me seemed insufficient for that day."

A certain lady lived for four years in the White House with President Lincoln's family. She gives the following incident of the sad days of 1863: —

"One day, Mr. Lincoln came into the room where I was fitting a dress on Mrs. Lincoln. His step was slow and heavy, and his face sad. Like a tired child he threw himself upon a sofa, and shaded his eyes with his hands. He was a complete picture of dejection. Mrs. Lincoln, observing his troubled look, asked —

"'Where have you been, father?'

"'To the War Department,' was the brief answer.

"'Any news?'

"'Yes, plenty of news, but no good news. It is dark, dark everywhere.'

"He reached forth one of his long arms and took a small Bible from a stand near the head of the sofa, opened the pages of the holy book, and was soon absorbed in reading them.

"A quarter of an hour passed, and, on glancing at the sofa, I saw that the face of the President seemed more cheerful. The dejected expression was gone, and the countenance seemed lighted up with new resolution and hope.

"The change was so marked that I could not but wonder at it, and wonder led to the desire to know what book of the Bible afforded so much comfort to the reader.

"Making the search for a missing article an excuse, I walked gently around the sofa, and, looking into the open book, I saw that Mr. Lincoln was reading that divine comforter, Job. He read with Christian eagerness, and the courage and hope that he derived from the inspired pages made him a new man.

"I almost imagined I could hear the Lord speaking to him from out the whirlwind of battle: 'Gird up now thy loins like a man; for I will demand of thee, and answer thou me.'

"What a sublime picture was this! The ruler of a mighty nation going to the pages of the Bible for comfort and courage — and finding both — in the darkest hours of his country's calamity."

No man but President Lincoln knew how great was the load of care which he bore, nor the amount of hard labor which he daily accomplished. With the usual perplexities of his great office, he carried the burdens of the Civil War, which he always called "this great trouble." Though the intellectual man had greatly grown, meantime, few people would recognize the hearty, blithesome, genial, and wiry Abraham Lincoln of earlier days, with his stooping figure, dull eyes, careworn face, and languid frame. The old, clear laugh never came back; his even temper was sometimes disturbed, and his natural charity for all was often turned into an unwonted suspicion of the motives of men, whose selfishness cost him so much wear of mind.

Lincoln did not have a hopeful temperament. Although he tried to look at the bright side of things, he was always prepared for disaster and defeat. He often saw success when others saw disaster; but oftener perceived a failure when others were elated with victory. He was never weary of commending the patience of the American people, which he thought something matchless and touching. He would often shed tears when speaking of the cheerful sacrifice of the light and strength of so many homes throughout the land. His own patience was marvellous. He was never crushed at defeat or unduly elated by success. Once he said the keenest blow of all the war was at an early stage, when the disaster at Ball's Bluff, and the death of his beloved friend, General Baker, smote upon him like a whirlwind from a desert.

Mr. Lincoln loved to read the humorous writers. He could repeat from memory whole chapters from the chronicler of the "Mackerel Brigade," Parson Nasby, and "Private Miles O'Reilly." These light trifles diverted his mind, or, as he said, gave him refuge from himself and his weariness. The Bible was a very familiar study, whole chapters of Isaiah, the New Testament, and the Psalms, being fixed in his memory. He liked the Old Testament best, and dwelt on the simple beauty of the historical books. Of the poets, he preferred Tom Hood and Holmes, the mixture of humor and pathos in their writings being attractive to him beyond all other poets.

The President's love of music was something passionate, but his tastes were simple and uncultivated, his choice being old airs, songs, and ballads, among which the plaintive Scotch songs were best liked. "Annie Laurie," and especially "Auld Robin Gray," never lost their charms for him.

He wrote slowly and with greatest deliberation, and liked to take his time; yet some of his despatches, written without any corrections, were models of compactness and finish. His private correspondence was extensive. He preferred writing his letters with his own hand, making copies himself frequently, and filing everything away in a set of pigeon-holes in his office. He conscientiously attended to his enormous correspondence, and read everything that appeared to demand his attention. Even in the busiest days of the war, the good President found time to send his autograph to every schoolboy who wrote to him for it.

"None of the artists or pictures," says Walt Whitman, "caught the deep, though subtle and indirect expression of Lincoln's face. There is something else there. One of the great portrait painters of two or three centuries ago is needed.

"Probably the reader has seen physiognomies (often old farmers, sea-captains, and such) that, behind their homeliness, or even ugliness, held superior points so subtle, yet so palpable, making the real life of their faces almost as impossible to depict as a wild perfume, or fruit-paste, or a passionate tone of the living voice — and such was Lincoln's face, the peculiar color, the lines of it, the eyes, mouth, expression. Of technical beauty it had nothing — but to the eye of a great artist it furnished a rare study, a feast and fascination."

Chapter 17

🔊

Barbara Fritchie

1766-1862

In December, 1766, a daughter was born in the house of a German immigrant, Nicolaus Hauer, in Lancaster, Pennsylvania, and she was named Barbara. She had four sisters and brothers. Their early years were spent in Pennsylvania and then the family moved to Frederick, Maryland.

Barbara went to school for a while in Baltimore. Her education was the best that could be obtained at that day, for she was "thoroughly well-read and could write." When she was ninety-two years old she scorned making her mark on business papers and proudly signed her name.

Barbara remembered the discussions that went on, when she was a very little girl, about the Boston tea party and the English taxes. She was nearly ten years old when the Declaration of Independence was signed. All her life long she talked with great pride of the success of the colonists. She remembered many scenes of the Revolution. Step by step she watched Washington's career and shared in the

Photograph of Barbara Fitchie

popular rejoicing when peace was announced. In 1791 Washington was entertained in Frederick and Barbara begged that her china be used in pouring the tea at the ball. And when Washington died and a memorial funeral was held in the town, she was chosen as one of the pall-bearers.

Frederick was a lovely little gem, set in a circle of historic hills, like Nazareth an old town with narrow streets and lanes, and houses with queer roofs where the shingles had a double lap that made them look like old Dutch tiles. There was a market square in the center of the town, and on the outskirts the stone barracks built during the reign of Queen Anne, where Braddock met Washington and Franklin in council, and where prisoners were kept during the Revolution.

Here lived Barbara Fritchie, an active capable woman, known for her sturdy good sense, her incessant industry and her intense loyalty to her country. Literally she grew with its growth, watching its progress through the War of 1812, the admission of new states, westward and ever westward expanding, till gold was discovered in California; and always the slavery question sinister and threatening in the background.

When Barbara was nearly forty she married John Caspar Fritchie, a glove maker. They lived in a little high-gabled story-and-a-half house on West Patrick Street, built of red brick penciled in white, with white shutters and two dormer windows in the long sloping roof. They owned two slaves, Nellie and Harry, who were so kindly treated that when freed they returned often, as children seek the home of their parents.

Her husband died in 1849 and Dame Fritchie, who never had any children, lived alone in the little house, busy with her many nieces and nephews, her knitting and her garden; a slight figure, under medium height, with small penetrating eyes, usually dressed in black alpaca or satin, with a starched muslin kerchief crossed on her breast, and a close white cap. She was always firm and decisive, and had indeed the reputation of a sharp tongue.

Then began the Civil War and Barbara, ninety-four years old, was noted for her fearless behavior and her intense outspoken loyalty, when loyalty was not the easiest matter in that border state. For Frederick had much to endure that winter. Soldiers of both armies were constantly in the way, skirmishes and duels were frequent in the narrow streets.

The flag was always flying from the Fritchie window and Dame Barbara kept busy, helping sick soldiers and cheering the despairing Unionists. "Never mind," she would say when news of reverses came, "we must conquer sometime." For stimulated by the glorious memory of what she had lived through, she had a supreme faith that the Union must survive. "It will never happen that one short life like mine shall see the beginning and the end of a nation like this." She would ask the shop-keeper, "How do matters look now?" If the reports were cheering her joy was evident; if sad, she would say, "Do not be cast down. We have seen darker times. Stand firm, it will all come right, I know it will. The Union must be preserved."

Often the southern troops marched through Frederick, tired out, and stopped to rest on the porches of private houses. Once they halted in front of Barbara Fritchie's home, sat on her steps, and went to the spring near by for water. To all this she made no objection, but when they began to talk in a derogatory way of her beloved country, she was at the door in a moment and bade them move on, laying about her with her cane in the most vigorous manner, crying, "Off, off, you Rebels!" and clearing the porch in a few moments.

With victory alternating between North and South, matters dragged on until September of 1862, when Lee's advance troops under Stonewall Jackson spent a week in Frederick, to encourage recruiting for the Confederate army. Every Union flag was ordered hauled down, and according to one version of the story Barbara Fritchie, with the other loyalists, took down her flag and hid it in the Bible, saying that no Rebel would think of looking for it there.

Another story tells how on the morning of the sixth Dame Barbara's niece went to see her and told her of a rumor that the soldiers would pass through the town that day. Presently the child ran in and called out in great excitement, "Aunt Fritchie, the troops are coming!"

To the loyal old lady troops meant only one army. She heard the sound of marching feet. Picking up a silk flag she stepped out on the porch and waved it at the men passing. Instantly a murmur arose. A captain, riding up to the porch, said kindly, "Granny, you had better take your flag in the house."

"I won't do it, I won't," was her reply, as she saw for the first time that the passing soldiers were

Barbara Fritchie, from *Poems of American Patriotism* by N.C. Wyeth

dressed in gray. Defiantly she shook the flag. The excitement in the ranks increased. Threatening murmurs arose. Another officer left the line and said, "Old woman, put that flag away, or you may get in trouble."

"I won't," she responded and waved it again.

Angry shouts came from the men. A third officer approaching warned her: "If you don't stop that, you'll have that flag shot out of your hand."

The captain, who was still standing near, turned to him and said angrily, "If you harm a hair of her head, I'll shoot you like a dog! March on," he commanded sternly, for some of the soldiers had lifted their guns.

On the twelfth of September the southerners left Frederick and the Union forces marched in, to leave the following day for South Mountain and Antietam. It was common talk among the northern soldiers that some old lady had kept a Union flag flying from her window during the Rebels' possession of the town, and that it had been fired on.

As the Federal troops were leaving the city General Reno noticed a crowd of people in front of Barbara Fritchie's home, reined in his horse and heard the story. On being told that she was more than ninety years old, he exclaimed, "The spirit of 1776!" and his men gave a mighty shout that echoed along the street. Some of the boys in blue ran to the window and grasped her hand, saying, "God bless you, old lady!" and "May you live long, you dear old soul!"

The general dismounted to shake hands with the aged heroine, who gave him some home-made currant wine, served in the blue delft from which Washington had drunk. He asked if she would sell him the flag. This she refused to do, but gave him a bunting flag.

"Frank," he said to his brother as they rode away, "whom does she remind you of?"

"Mother."

The general nodded his head. The next day Reno fell at South Mountain, mortally wounded, and Barbara's flag was placed on his casket when it was sent north to his Massachusetts home.

Three months later Dame Fritchie died, at four-score and sixteen, and was buried in the little graveyard of the Reformed Church in Frederick.

Her story was published in the newspapers and gained credence in Maryland and in Washington. It was accepted as a fitting symbol of a real and great emotion of the people. Mrs. Southworth, the novelist, hearing it from friends and from a neighbor who was a connection of the Fritchie family, sent it to Whittier, adding, "This story of a woman's heroism seemed as much to belong to you as a book picked up with your autograph on the fly-leaf."

Within a fortnight after its receipt the Quaker poet, in his most heroic mood, wrote his Barbara Fritchie ballad, remarkable for its lofty patriotism. Though he had no military training his lines are full of the spirit of army life, the tread of marching soldiers, the orders short and sharp, a stirring setting for the courageous act of an old lady of ninety-six.

"It ought to have fallen into better hands," Whittier wrote to Mrs. Southworth. "If it is good for anything thee deserves the credit of it."

The poem was sent to the *Atlantic Monthly*, whose editor replied, "Enclosed is a check for fifty dollars, but Barbara's weight should be in gold!"

The ballad was, and is, most popular through the North, for it belongs in the class which the world will never willingly let die. But it aroused great enmity in the South where people bitterly resented the statement that a favorite general had ordered his men to fire on an old lady. There were many denials of all the details of the story, some from members of the Fritchie family—that Jackson did not pass the Fritchie house, proved by statements from his staff; that Barbara had waved her flag only to welcome the Union army, and the incident had been blended with the story of Mrs. Quantrell, a loyal school-teacher who did wave the flag in sight of the Confederates; that no such person as Barbara Fritchie had ever lived in Frederick!

Said Whittier years later, "There has been a good deal of dispute about my little poem. That there was a Dame Fritchie in Frederick who loved the old flag is not disputed by any one. If I made any mistake in the details there was none in my estimate of her noble character and her loyalty and patriotism. If there was no such occurrence, so much the worse for Frederick City."

Across the town from the little churchyard where John and Barbara Fritchie lie buried is the monument marking the grave of the author of The Star-spangled Banner. And in both cemeteries the flag floats out, signaling the one to the other, fulfilling the lines of the Quaker poet:

"Over Barbara Fritchie's grave
Flag of freedom and union, wave!
And ever the stars above look down
On thy stars below in Frederick town."

Chapter 18

❧

The Surrender at Appomattox

From General Grant's Personal Memoirs
April 9, 1865

Before stating what took place between General Lee and myself, I will give all there is of the story of the famous apple-tree. Wars produce many stories of fiction, some of which are told until they are believed to be true. The war of the rebellion was no exception to this rule; and the story of the apple-tree is one of those fictions based on a slight foundation of fact.

There was an apple orchard on the side of the hill occupied by the Confederate forces. Running diagonally up the hill was a wagon road, which, at one point, ran very near one of the trees, so that the wheels of vehicles had, on that side, cut off the roots of this tree, leaving a little embankment. General Babcock, of my staff, reported to me that when he first met General Lee he was sitting upon this embankment, with his feet in the road below and his back resting against the tree. The story has no other foundation than that. Like many other stories, it would be very good if it was only true.

I had known General Lee in the old army, and had served with him in the Mexican War, but did not suppose, owing to the difference in our age and rank, that he would remember me; while I would more naturally remember him distinctly, because he was the chief of staff of General Scott in the Mexican War.

When I had left camp that morning I had not expected so soon the result that was then taking place, and consequently was in rough garb. I was without a sword, as I usually was when on horse-back on the field, and wore a soldier's blouse for a coat, with the shoulder-straps of my rank to indicate to the army who I was. When I went into the house I found General Lee. We greeted each other, and after shaking hands took our seats. I had my staff with me, a good portion of whom were in the room during the whole of the interview.

What General Lee's feelings were I do not know. As he was a man of much dignity, with an impassible face, it was impossible to say whether he felt inwardly glad that the end had finally come, or felt sad over the result, and was too manly to show it. Whatever his feelings, they were entirely concealed from my observation; but my own feelings, which had been quite jubilant on the receipt of his letter, were sad and depressed. I felt like anything than rejoicing at the downfall of a foe who had fought so long and valiantly, and had suffered so much for a cause, though that was, I believe, one of the worst for which a people ever fought, and one for which there was the least excuse. I do not question, however, the sincerity of the great mass of those who were opposed to us. General Lee was dressed in a full uniform which was entirely new, and was wearing a sword of considerable value, very likely the sword which had been presented by the State of Virginia; at all events, it was an entirely different sword from the one that would ordinarily be worn in the field. In my rough travelling

Surrender Scene Inside the McLean House, by Louis Mathieu Guillaume, 1892

suit, the uniform of a private, with the straps of a lieutenant-general, I must have contrasted very strongly with a man so handsomely dressed, six feet high, and of a faultless form. But this was not a matter that I thought of until afterwards.

We soon fell into a conversation about old army times. He remarked that he remembered me very well in the old army; and I told him that as a matter of course I remembered him perfectly. Our conversation grew so pleasant that I almost forgot the object of our meeting. General Lee called my attention to the object of our meeting, and said that he had asked for this interview for the purpose of getting from me the terms I proposed to give his army. I said that I meant merely that his army should lay down their arms, not to take them up again during the war unless duly and properly exchanged. He said that he had so understood my letter, and that the terms I proposed to give his army ought to be written out. I then began writing out the terms. When I put my pen to paper I did not know the first word that I should make use of, I only knew what was in my mind, and that I wished to express it clearly so that there could be no mistaking it. As I wrote on, the thought occurred to me that the officers had their own private horses and effects, which were important to them, but of no value to us: also that it would be unnecessary humiliation to call upon them to deliver their side-arms.

No conversation, not one word, passed between General Lee and myself, either about private property, side-arms, or kindred subjects. When he read over that part of the terms about side-arms, horses, and private property of the officers, he remarked – with some feeling, I thought – that this would have a happy effect upon the army. I then said to him that I thought this would be about the last battle of the war – I sincerely hoped so; and I said further, I took it that most of the men in the ranks were small farmers. The whole country had been so raided by the two armies that it was doubtful whether they would be able to put in a crop to carry themselves and their families through the next winter without the aid of the horses they were then riding. The United States did not want them, and I would therefore instruct the officers I left behind to receive the paroles of his troops to let every man who claimed to own a horse or mule take the animal to his home. Lee remarked again that this would have a happy effect.

The much-talked-of surrendering of Lee's sword and my handing it back, this and much more that has been said about it is the purest romance. The word sword or side-arms was not mentioned by either of us until I wrote it in the terms. General Lee, after all was completed and before taking his leave, remarked that his army was in a very bad condition for want of food, and that they were without forage; and that his men had been living for some days on parched corn exclusively, and that he would have to ask me for rations and forage. I told him "certainly," and asked for how many men he wanted rations. His answer was, "About twenty-five thousand." I authorized him to send his own commissary and quartermaster to Appomattox Station, where he could have all the provisions wanted. Lee and I then separated as cordially as we had met, he returning to his own men, and all went into bivouac for the night at Appomattox.

When the news of the surrender first reached our lines, our men commenced firing a salute of a hundred guns, in honor of the victory. I at once sent word, however, to have it stopped; the Confederates were now our prisoners, and we did not want to exult over their downfall.

Chapter 19

ℰᴑ

Dorothea Dix

1802-1887

Dorothea Dix has been called "the most useful and distinguished woman America has yet produced." Let us follow the events of her life and decide for ourselves whether this statement is true.

Dorothea Lynde Dix was born April 4, 1802, at Hampden, Maine. Her father, Joseph Dix, was a man of unstable character and of a most singular mental make-up. In fact, he was regarded as almost insane on religious questions. He wandered about from place to place writing and publishing tracts, spending in this way the little money he had, without regard to the needs of his family. His wife and children were required to assist in the stitching and pasting of the tracts, a tiresome work which brought them no return.

At twelve years of age Dorothea rebelled against this labor. She wished to attend school, but there was little chance for her to study while she lived with her father. So she ran away from Worcester, where the family then lived, and went to Boston, the home of her grandmother, Mrs. Dorothea Lynde Dix.

Oil painting of Dorothea Lynde Dix, by Samuel Bell Waugh, 1868

Mrs. Dix received the girl as kindly as her nature would permit. But she was a stern woman, with very strict ideas of training children, and every piece of work done for her had to be perfectly performed or severe punishment followed.

Once, when little Dorothea had failed to accomplish a task as well as her grandmother thought she should, she was compelled to spend a whole week alone without speaking to anyone. This

84

sounds cruel, but Dorothea's grandmother wished to make the child careful and painstaking.

Poor little Dorothea! She said in after years that she "never knew childhood." But she submitted to her grandmother's sternness rather than return to her father and the wandering, useless life he led. She had always in mind the day when she would be able to support herself and help her younger brothers. So she studied diligently, and being clever, made great progress. When she was fourteen, she returned to Worcester, where she opened a small school for young children. In order to look old enough for a teacher, she lengthened the skirts of her dresses and arranged her hair grown-woman fashion.

The school succeeded, for Dorothea, though always kind and gentle, was a strict disciplinarian. The year following, she returned to Boston and studied to fit herself for more advanced work in teaching. In 1821, when she was nineteen years of age, she opened a day and boarding school in that city, in a house belonging to her grandmother. Here she received pupils from the best families in Boston and the neighboring towns, and was able to send for her brothers and educate them, while supporting herself. Dorothea's sympathies, meanwhile, were drawn to the poor children about her, who had no means of obtaining an education because their parents could not afford to pay the tuition. She put the matter before her austere grandmother, and begged for the use of a loft over the stable for a school room for these children. The little "barn school" was the beginning of a movement that grew, and later resulted in the Warren Street Chapel.

You may imagine how happy Dorothea Dix was now — to be self-supporting and to be helping others to become so! She managed the two schools, had the care of her two brothers, and took entire charge of her grandmother's home. For Mrs. Dix had learned to admire and trust the granddaughter whom she had once found so careless.

This amount of work would completely fill the lives of most people, yet Dorothea found time to prepare a text-book upon *Common Things*. Sixty editions of the book were printed and sold. It was followed by two others: *Hymns for Children* and *Evening Hours*.

In order to do all this work, she arose early and sat up late into the night. Naturally her health failed under such a strain. After six years she gave up her schools, and took a position as governess in a family living at Portsmouth, Rhode Island. Here she lived much in the open air, and her great desire for universal knowledge led her to make a special study of botany and marine life.

Her health failing again, she visited Philadelphia, and then went South as far as Alexandria, Virginia, writing short stories the while to support herself. The winter of 1830 she spent in the West Indies with the family of Dr. Channing. There she at last regained her health.

The following spring. Miss Dix returned to Boston, and reopened her school in the old Dix homestead. Pupils flocked to her, and for five years the work flourished. Her influence over her pupils was wonderful. They thought her very beautiful, as indeed she was. Mrs. Livermore writes of her: "Miss Dix was slight and delicate in appearance. She must have been beautiful in her youth and was still very sweet looking, with a soft voice, graceful figure and winning manners."

In 1836, ill health obliged her to close her school once more. This time she went to England. Though only thirty-four, she had saved enough money to enable her to live in comfort without labor. Shortly after, her grandmother died, leaving her enough to carry out the plans for helping others, which had become a part of her life. She then returned from England and made her home in Washington.

In 1841, however, we find her again in Boston and at this time her real life-work began. It happened that a minister well known to Miss Dix had charge of a Sunday school in the East Cambridge jail. He needed a teacher to take charge of a class of twenty women, and asked Miss Dix if she could tell him of any suitable person.

Miss Dix thought the matter over and then said, "I will take the class myself!"

Her friends objected because of her frail health, but having once arrived at a decision, Dorothea Dix never changed her mind. As one of her pupils said, "Fixed as fate, we considered her!"

The following Sunday, after the session was over, she went into the jail and talked with many of the prisoners. It seemed that they had many righteous grievances, one being that no heat of any kind was provided for their cells.

When Miss Dix asked the keeper of the jail to heat the rooms, he replied that the prisoners did not need heat, and that besides, stoves would be unsafe. Though she begged him to do something to make the cells more comfortable, he refused. She then brought the case before the Court in East Cambridge. The Court granted her request and heat was furnished the prisoners.

In the East Cambridge jail she saw many things too horrible to believe. The cells were dirty, the inmates crowded together in poorly ventilated quarters, the sane and insane often being placed in the same room. These conditions, and others too sad to mention, she made public through the newspapers and the pulpits. But she did not stop at this. Every jail and almshouse in Massachusetts was visited by her; she must see for herself how the unfortunate inmates were treated. For two years she traveled about, visiting these institutions and taking notes. Then she prepared her famous Memorial to the Legislature.

In this Memorial Miss Dix said: "I proceed, gentlemen, briefly to call your attention to the present state of insane persons within this Commonwealth, in cages, closets, cellars, stalls, pens, chained and naked, beaten with rods and lashed into obedience." Proofs were offered for all facts stated.

The Memorial was presented by Dr. S. G. Howe, husband of Julia Ward Howe. Dr. Howe was then a member of the Legislature. The conditions thus made public shocked the entire community, so that, after much discussion, a bill was passed enlarging the asylum at Worcester. A small beginning, yet the grand work of reform was started, and Miss Dix was grateful.

She then turned her attention to other States, visiting the jails, almshouses, and insane asylums as far west as Illinois and as far south as Louisiana. In Rhode Island she found the insane shockingly treated.

At that time there lived in Providence a very rich man named Butler. He had never been known to give anything to help the unfortunate, but Miss Dix decided to appeal to him. People smiled when they heard that she intended to call upon Mr. Butler and ask him for money.

During the call, he talked of everything except the subject nearest Miss Dix's heart, "talking against time," as they say, to prevent her from putting the vital question. At length she said in a quiet but forceful manner:

"*Mr. Butler, I wish you to hear what I have to say.* I bring before you certain facts involving terrible suffering to your fellow creatures, suffering you can relieve."

She then told him what she had seen.

Mr. Butler heard her story to the end without interruption. Then he said, "What do you want me to do?"

"I want you to give $50,000 to enlarge the insane hospital in this city!"

"Madam, I'll do it!" was the reply.

After three years of this sort of work, Miss Dix became an expert on the question of how an insane asylum should be built and managed. In New Jersey, she succeeded after much hard work in securing the passage of a bill establishing the New Jersey State Lunatic Asylum, and the money necessary to build it. This building was a model for the times.

For twelve years she went up and down through the United States in the interests of the suffering insane, securing the enlargement of three asylums and the building of thirteen.

In 1850, Miss Dix secured the passage of a bill giving twelve million acres of public lands for the benefit of the poor insane, the deaf and dumb, and the blind. Applause went up all over the country, yet, strange to say, after the passage of the bill by both Houses, President Franklin Pierce vetoed it!

This was a severe blow to Miss Dix and she again went to Europe for a rest. But rest she could not. All the large European cities had abuses of this kind to be corrected, and she must work to help them.

A most interesting story is told of her encounter with Pope Pius IX. In vain had she tried to get authority in Rome to enable her to do something to improve the horrible Italian prisons. She had even tried, but vainly, to get audience with the Pope. One day she saw his carriage, *stopped it,* and addressed him, willy-nilly, in *Latin,* as she knew no Italian. Her enterprise appears to have impressed the Pope favorably, for he gave her everything she asked for. In her own country, again, she extended her labors to the Western States. Then the breaking out of the Civil War rendered such labors useless.

But now there were the soldiers to help! Her active interest in them came about in the following way:

Shortly after April, 1861, she happened to be passing through Baltimore when the Sixth Regiment of Massachusetts, on its way to Washington, was stoned by a vast mob, several men being killed. At once Miss Dix knew what to do. She took the first train she could get for Washington, and reported at the War Department for free service in the hospitals, where through Secretary Simon Cameron, she immediately received the appointment as "Superintendent of Women Nurses." Here, truly, was an enormous piece of work for her.

Among her duties were the selection and assignment of women nurses; the superintendence of the thousands of women already serving; the seeing that supplies were fairly distributed; and looking after the proper care of wounded soldiers. Her remarkable executive ability soon brought order and system out of confusion. It is said that she accepted no women who were under thirty years of age, and demanded that they be plain in dress and without beauty. Good health and good moral character were also, of course, requirements.

Many of the surgeons and nurses disliked her. They said she was severe, that she would not listen to any advice nor take any suggestions. The real cause of her unpopularity, however, was that she demanded of all about her entire unselfishness and strict devotion to work. Very severe was she with careless nurses or rough surgeons.

Two houses were rented by her to hold the supplies sent to her care, and still other houses were rented for convalescent soldiers or nurses who needed rest. She employed two secretaries, owned ambulances and kept them busy, printed and distributed circulars, settled disputes in matters which concerned her nurses, took long journeys when necessary, and paid from her own private purse many expenses incurred. Everything she possessed — fortune, time, strength — she gave to her country in its time of need.

During the four years of the War, Miss Dix never took a holiday. Often she had to be reminded of her meals, so interested was she in the work. At the close of the War, when the Hon. Edwin M. Stanton, then Secretary of War, asked her how the nation could best thank her for her services, she answered, "I would like a flag."

Two beautiful flags were given to her with a suitable inscription. These flags she bequeathed to Harvard College, and they now hang over the doors of Memorial Hall.

The War over, Miss Dix again took up her work for the insane and for fifteen years more devoted herself to their welfare.

In 1881, at the age of seventy-nine, she retired to the hospital she had been the means of building at Trenton, New Jersey, and here she was tenderly cared for until her death in 1887.

Chapter 20

❧

The Sanitary Commission

On the 13th of April, 1861, Fort Sumter in Charleston harbor was fired upon by the soldiers of the South.

This was the beginning of the great struggle known in history as the Civil War in America.

Two days before this, Abraham Lincoln called for seventy-five thousand men to defend the government and maintain its laws in the South.

The call was answered at once and with great enthusiasm. Not only did seventy-five thousand men offer themselves, but thousands more who could not be accepted. Business was at a stand-still. The plow was left in the furrow. The factory doors were closed. The thoughts of all men were upon the crisis which the country was facing. In every village of the North the tap of the drum and the shrill music of the fife were heard.

On the very day that Lincoln issued his call, some women of Bridgeport, Connecticut, met together to consider what they could do.

"We cannot go to war," they said, "but our husbands and sons can go — yes, they will go. Shall we who remain at home be idle?"

"There will be bloodshed," said some.

"And there will be much suffering in camp and on the march," said others. "Men will be wounded in battle, they will be sick from exposure, they will need better attention than the army surgeons alone can give them. Can we not do something to help? "

And so these earnest, sympathetic women of Bridgeport organized themselves into what they called a Soldiers' Aid Society, and resolved to do all that they could for the relief and comfort of the men who were at that moment hurrying forward to answer the President's call.

"We cannot fight," they said, "but we can help the fighters."

Miss Almena Bates, a young lady of Charlestown, Massachusetts, did not know what the ladies of Bridgeport were doing, but she started out that same day to do something herself. She went with pencil and paper to her friends and acquaintances and asked each one to volunteer as a helper.

"The boys are answering the President's call," she said. "Tomorrow they will be on their way to the front. There will be war. Nurses will be needed on the battlefields and in the hospitals. Medicines, food, little comforts for the sick and wounded — all these ought to be ready at the first need. What will you do?"

In a few days women in every part of the North were forming aid societies. But as yet it was hard for them to accomplish very much. So long as each little society was working alone, there was no certainty that the intended help would ever reach the right place.

At length, two months after the fall of Fort Sumter, a great organization was formed that would extend all over the North and would include the aid societies. The president of this organization was Rev. Henry W. Bellows of New York, and many well-known men and women were among its members.

Some people shook their heads and hung back.

"The government will provide for the relief and comfort of the soldiers in the field," they said. "What is the use of these aid societies and this great organization?"

Even President Lincoln at first said that he thought the association would prove to be like a fifth wheel to a coach — very much in the way.

But the war had now begun in terrible earnest. In the camps and on the battlefield, the soldiers were learning what was meant by privation and suffering. The plans for the work of the association were carefully made out by Dr. Bellows and his assistants, and were submitted to the government. The president approved them. And thus the United States Sanitary Commission, as it was called, was given the authority to go forward with its great work of caring for the health and comfort of the soldiers.

From the aid societies and from the people at large, help was freely sent. Fairs were held all over the country for the purpose of raising money. Men, women, and children joined in working. Each

"Our Women and the War," by Winslow Homer in Harper's Weekly, 1862

town and city tried to do more than its neighbor had done. At one fair in Chicago more than seventy-five thousand dollars was raised. The people of the state of New York gave nearly a million dollars for the cause.

President Lincoln wrote: "Amongst the extraordinary manifestations of this war, none has been more remarkable than these fairs. And their chief agents are the women of America. I am not accustomed to the use of the language of eulogy; but I must say, that if all that has been said by orators and poets since the creation of the world in praise of women were applied to the women of America, it would not do them justice for their conduct during this war. God bless the women of America!"

Not only did these women form societies, hold fairs, and give of their means for this cause, but many of them were active in the work itself. Women of culture and education, accustomed to all the comforts that wealth can give, went to the front as nurses and as directors of relief in the hospitals and on the battlefield. First among these was Dorothea Dix, who, within two weeks after the president's call for volunteers, received the public thanks of the surgeon general and was placed in charge of all the women nurses at the front.

Among those who likewise gave their time and energies to this noble work were Mrs. Julia Ward Howe, Mrs. Mary A. Livermore, Clara Barton, Dr. Mary Walker, and many others scarcely less distinguished. Of the golden deeds done by these self-sacrificing women, there is no adequate record save in the book of that angel who writes the names of those who love mankind.

There were hundreds, also, of humble workers who were no less earnest in their efforts to do good. These were the nurses in the hospitals and in the field, besides numberless others who labored at home for the support of the Commission.

The direct caring for the sick and wounded was only a small portion of the duties performed under the direction of the Commission. To prevent disease was one of the first objects, for disease alone might cause the defeat, if not the destruction, of our armies.

Hence, the managers were on the watch for whatever was likely to guard or improve the health of the soldiers at the front. They saw that the food was wholesome and that it was properly cooked.

They started truck gardens for supplying vegetables to the men. They had charge of the ice and other luxuries for the sick. They looked after the wounded who were sent to the rear. They collected bedding, clothing, and all sorts of delicacies for the use of the sick. They wrote letters for the disabled, and gave them stationery, stamps, and envelopes. They gathered up books and newspapers for the men to read while sick or off duty. They furnished lodging for the mothers and wives who had come to the hospital or the camp on errands of mercy to their wounded sons or husbands. Lastly, they helped the men who for any reason had been discharged and lacked the means or the ability to reach their homes.

The war continued four years.

During that time more than fifteen million dollars in supplies of various kinds, besides nearly five million dollars in money, was freely given for the cause by the generous-hearted people of the North. Of those who were engaged in doing the work of the Commission, many served without pay and without desire of reward. Others, however, performed their duties from more selfish motives — some for the wages which they received, some for the profits which they hoped to derive through less honorable channels. These last deserve no commendation, although they may have done some valuable service. Their deeds were not golden.

But think of the truly golden deeds that were done in connection with this cause. Think of the men whose lives were saved. Think of the mothers and wives who were made happy by the care bestowed upon their loved ones, enabling them finally to return to their homes. Think of the thousands of benefits that were performed through this one agency. Who is there so lacking in noble impulses as to deny that it is more heroic to save life than to destroy it?

Chapter 21

❧

Clara Barton

1821-1912

Clarissa Harlowe Barton was born on December twenty-fifth, in an old farm-house in Worcester County, Massachu-setts. Her grandfather had fought through the Revolution, her father in Mad Anthony Wayne's campaigns against the Indians. Clara listened to many a stirring story of the dangers they had met as they fought their battles over again, she learned her country's history and loved it passion-ately.

The older Barton children were her teachers and very rapidly indeed she learned. For she went to school at three, able to spell words of three syllables, but so shy she could not answer questions. Her athletic brother David, whom she admired greatly, taught her to ride.

"Learning to ride is just learning a horse," said he.

"How can I learn a horse?" asked the little sister.

"Just feel the horse a part of yourself, the big half for the time being. Here, hold fast by the mane," and David lifted her up to a colt's back, sprang on another himself and away they galloped down the pasture a mad ride which they repeated often, till she learned to stick on. In after years when she rode strange horses in a trooper's sad-dle, for all-night gallops to safety, she was grateful to David for those wild rides

Photograph of Clara Barton

93

among the colts.

Strong in body, alert in mind, Clara Barton grew up, never free from shyness unless she was busily at work. "The only real fun is doing things," she would say. She helped milk and churn, she learned to drive a nail straight, to deal with a situation efficiently, with quick decision. When she was eleven David was seriously injured by a fall from the roof of a new barn, and was for two years an invalid. At once Clara took charge, her love and sympathy expressed in untiring service. In a moment she was changed from a lively child, fond of outdoor sports, to a nurse calm and cheerful, full of resources, no matter how exacting the doctors' orders were, no matter how much David was suffering. The sickroom was tidy and quiet. Clara was clear-headed, equal to every emergency, always at her post, nothing too hard for her to do well and promptly, if it would make her brother more comfortable. For those two years she had not even one half-holiday, so her apprenticeship was thoroughly served.

"That child's a born nurse," the neighbors would say. And the doctors, agreeing, praised her tenderness and patience. Years later thousands of men echoed David's words when he spoke of her loving care.

But these two years made her more sensitive and self-conscious. Her shyness and unhappiness made her a real problem to her mother.

"Give her some responsibility," advised a wise family friend, "give her a school to teach. For others she will be fearless."

Far ahead of girls of her age in her studies, at fifteen Clara Barton put up her hair and lengthened her skirts and went to face her forty pupils. "It was one of the most awful moments of my life," she described it long afterward. "I could not find my voice, my hand trembled so I was afraid to turn the page. But the end of that first day proved I could do it."

Her pluck and strength won the respect of the big rough boys, who tried her out on the playground and found she was as sturdy as they. That school was a great success, and for sixteen years she taught, winter and summer.

In Bordentown, New Jersey, no school was possible, she heard, because of the lawless children who ran wild on the streets. The town officials were convinced it was hopeless, no use to make the experiment. Here was something to be done, it challenged her!

"Give me three months, and I'll teach for nothing," she proposed, her eyes flashing with determination.

In a tumbledown old building she began with six gamins, each of whom at the end of the day became an enthusiastic advertisement for the new teacher. At the close of the school year she had an assistant, six hundred children on the roll, and a fine new building was erected, the first public school in the state. For Clara Barton had a gift for teaching, plus a pioneer zeal.

When her voice gave out she went to Washington for a rest and secured a position in the patent office. So she was at the capital when the conflict long threatening between North and South developed into civil war. Sumter was fired on. The time for sacrifice had come.

In response to Lincoln's call for volunteers Massachusetts sent men immediately, and on the historic nineteenth of April one regiment was attacked in the streets of Baltimore by a furious mob. With a good many wounded their train finally reached Washington and was met by a number of sympathetic women, Clara Barton among them. In the group of injured soldiers she recognized some

Earliest known photograph of Clara Barton

of her old pupils and friends. At the infirmary she helped dress their wounds. Nothing was ready for such an emergency. Handkerchiefs gave out. Women rushed to their homes and tore up sheets for bandages. This was Clara Barton's first experience in caring for wounded soldiers.

She wanted them to have the necessities, and all the comforts possible. So she put an advertisement in a Worcester paper, asking for supplies and money for the wounded men of the sixth regiment, and stating that she would receive and give out whatever was sent. Overwhelming was the response of Massachusetts. The food and clothing filled her apartment to overflowing and she had to rent space in a warehouse.

This work made a new person of the shy Clara Barton who had been a bundle of fears. This was no time to be self-conscious. Here was a great need, and she knew that she had the ability to meet it.

South of Washington battles were going on. Transports left each day with provisions for the army of the Potomac, returning with a load of wounded soldiers. Clara Barton went to the docks to meet them. She moved about, bandaging here, giving medicine there, feeding those weak from the long fighting and lack of nourishment, writing letters home, sick at heart when she saw men who had lain on the damp ground for hours, whose fever had set in, for whom her restoratives and dressings and tender care were too late.

If only wounds could be attended to as soon as the soldiers fell in battle, she knew that hundreds of deaths could be prevented. She must go to the front, to the very firing line, though it was against all tradition, against all army regulations, against public sentiment. For many weeks she met only rebuffs and refusals, always the same reply: "No, the battle-field is no place for a woman. It is full of danger!"

True but how great was the need of the men at the front, how great the need of each soldier's life for the nation! Help must be brought to them when they fell. She laid her plan before her father who said, "If you believe that it is your duty, you must go to the front. You need not fear harm. Every true soldier will respect and bless you."

Without a doubt then she determined to persist until she received permission. At last she was able to put her request to Assistant-Quartermaster General Rucker and asked him for a pass to the battle front.

"I have the stores, give me a way to reach the men."

"But you must think of the dangers this work will bring you. At any time you may be under the fire of the enemy's guns."

"But," was her answer, "I am the daughter of a soldier, I am not afraid of the battle-field." She described to him the condition of many of the men when they reached Washington and added earnestly, "I must go to the front, to care for them quickly."

The passport was given her and through the weary years of the war she stayed at her post giving medicine to the sick, stimulants to the wounded and dying, nourishing food to men faint from loss of blood. Working under no society or leader she was free to come and go. On sixteen battle-fields, during the hot, muggy summer days of the long siege of Charleston, all through the Wilderness campaign, in the Richmond hospitals, there was no limit to her service. And from her first day on the firing line she had the confidence of the officers and their help and encouragement. Wherever there were wounded soldiers who had been under her care, Clara Barton's name was spoken with affection and with tears.

In as far as was possible, word of coming engagements was sent her in advance, that she might be ready with her supplies. At Antietam while shot was whizzing thick around the group of workers, she ordered her wagons driven to an old farmhouse just back of the lines. Between the tall rows of corn, into the barnyard, the worst cases were carried. For lack of medical supplies the surgeons were using bandages of cornhusks.

Her supplies quickly unloaded, Clara Barton hurried out to revive the wounded, giving them bread soaked in wine. The store of bread ran out, she had left only three cases of wine. "Open them," she commanded, "give us that, and God help us all!" for faster and faster soldiers were coming in. She watched the men open the cases. What was that around the bottles? Cornmeal! She looked at it closely; yes, finely ground and sifted. It could not have been worth more if it had been gold dust. In the farmhouse they found kettles. She mixed the cornmeal with water and soon was making great quantities of gruel. All night long they carried this hot food up and down the rows of wounded soldiers.

On one of these trips, in the twilight, she met a surgeon tired and disheartened. He had only one short candle left, and if men's lives

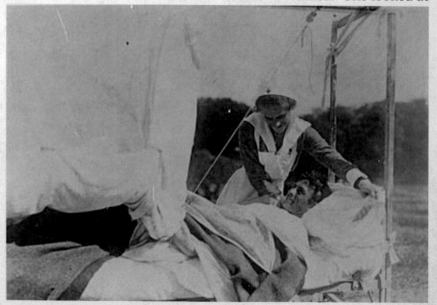

Clara Barton in Theater of Operations

were to be saved, the doctors must work all night. "Heartless neglect and carelessness," he stormed. But Miss Barton had four boxes of candles in her stores, ready for just such an emergency.

Near that battle-field she remained until all her supplies were gone. "If we had had more wagons," she reported to General Rucker, "there would have been enough for all the cases at Antietam."

"You shall have enough the next time," he responded. And the government, recognizing the value of her service, gave her ten wagons and sixty mules and drivers.

Her work succeeded because she had initiative and practical judgment and rare executive ability and the power of managing men. When her drivers were rebellious and sulky, showing little respect for orders that put them under a woman, she controlled them just as she had the rough boys in her school. Once she prepared a hot dinner and asked them to share it. After she had cleared away the dishes and was sitting alone by the fire, awkward and self-conscious they came up to her.

"Come and get warm," she welcomed them.

"No'm, we didn't come for that," said the leader. "We come to tell you we're ashamed. Truth is, lady, we didn't want to come. We knew there was fightin' ahead, an' we ain't never seen a train with a woman in charge. Now we've been mean and contrary all day long, and here you've treated us like we was the general and his staff, and it's the best meal we've had in two years and we shan't trouble you again."

The next morning they brought her a steaming hot breakfast and for six months remained with her, through battles and camps and marches, through frost and snow and heat, a devoted corps of assistants, always ready for her orders. They helped her nurse the sick and dress the wounded and soothe the dying, and day by day they themselves grew gentler and kinder and more tender.

Once Clara Barton worked for five days and nights with three hours of sleep. Once she had a narrow escape from capture. Often in danger it seemed as though she had a special protection that she might save the lives of others. Stooping to give a wounded soldier a drink of water, a bullet whizzed between them, tearing a hole in her sleeve and ending the boy's life.

She gave her help to men who had fought on either side. They were suffering, they needed her, that was enough. No man is your enemy when he is wounded. She leaned over a dying officer in a hospital; a Confederate looked up into her kind face and whispered: "You have been so very good to me. Do not cross the river, our men are leading you into an ambush. You must save yourself."

But his warning was unheeded when later that day the hero-surgeon who was opening an emergency dressing-station across the river, asked her help. She went over to Fredericksburg where every stone wall was a blazing line of battle. A regiment came marching down the street. She stepped aside. Thinking she must be a terrified southerner, left behind in their hurried flight, the general leaned from his saddle to ask: "You're alone and in great danger, madam. Do you want protection?"

"Thank you, but I think" – Clara Barton looked up at the ranks of soldiers marching past – "I think, sir, I'm the best protected woman in the United States!"

"That's so, that's so," cried out the men and gave her a great cheer that was taken up by line after line till it sounded like the cheering after a victory.

"I believe you're right, madam," said the general, bowing low, and galloped away.

Over the battle-field a sharp wind was blowing. The suffering men lay shivering and half frozen in the bitter cold. Some were found famished under the snow. Clara Barton had all the wounded brought to one place and great fires built up. But that was not heat enough to warm them. What to do? She discovered an old chimney not far away. "Tear it down," she ordered, "heat the bricks and place them around the men." Soon she had kettles of coffee and gruel steaming over the fires, and many a life she saved at Fredericksburg.

As the war drew to an end President Lincoln received hundreds and hundreds of letters from anxious parents asking for news of their boys. The list of missing totaled sixty thousand. In despair the president sent for Miss Barton, thinking she had more information than any one else, and asked her to take up the task. A four years' task it proved to be. She copied infirmary and burial lists. She studied records of prisons and hospitals. At Andersonville she laid out the national cemetery and identified nearly thirteen thousand graves. She succeeded in tracing and sending definite word of thirty thousand men. From Maine to Virginia the soldiers knew her. Through the whole country her name became a household word.

Her strong will had held her body to its work during the long war and for this tracing service afterward. Then the doctors insisted she must rest and sent her to Switzerland for change of scene. After a month when she was beginning to feel some improvement, she had callers one day representing the International Red Cross Society.

"What is that?" asked Clara Barton.

And they explained how a Swiss, visiting the battle-field of Solferino and seeing thousands of French and Austrians wounded, inadequately cared for, had planned a society for the relief of soldiers. Its badge, a red cross on a white ground, would give its workers protection from both armies, and they would help all persons without regard to their race or religion or uniform exactly the principle on which she had been working, and to-day the very heart of the Red Cross plan. Already, they said, the society was formed and twenty-two nations had joined it. But the United States, though invited twice, had done nothing. They asked her help.

Three days afterward the Franco-Prussian War began and soon Clara Barton was again at the front. With the German army she entered Strasburg after the siege. On every hand were sick and wounded soldiers, women and children homeless and ragged and starving. Relief work started, she went to Paris on the outbreak of the revolution there. And this work made her enthusiastic about the Red Cross. For at once she felt the difference she saw the new society accomplish in four months, with system and trained workers, what our country had failed to do in four years. What a contrast supplies in plenty, wounds dressed at once, cleanliness, comfort, wherever the white flag with the red cross was flying, instead of mistakes, delays, needless suffering, lives sacrificed. She said to herself, "If I live to return to America, I will try to make them understand what the Red Cross and the Geneva Treaty mean."

She succeeded, though it was a task of years. She found officials indifferent, hard to convince, clinging to the tradition and prejudice that forbade any alliance with foreign countries, and saying, "Why make plans for another war? We'll never have it!"

But in March, 1882, the treaty was signed. Clara Barton became the first president of the American Red Cross Society, an office she held for twenty-two years. It was her suggestion that they be prepared to meet any emergency and give relief in time of peace as well as war. It was her influence that carried this American amendment in the International Red Cross Congress.

Many have been the calamities where the Red Cross has given aid two wars, floods in the Ohio and Mississippi Rivers, the Texas famine, the Charleston earthquake, the disaster at San Francisco, Florida's yellow fever, the Johnstown flood, forest fires – these are a few of the urgent calls in our own land; and abroad the sufferers in the Russian and Chinese famines, in Armenia and South Africa, bear witness to her care.

Eighty years old, she went herself to Galveston. At seventy-seven McKinley sent her to carry relief to the starving Cubans. And during the Spanish War she nursed American and Cuban and Spanish soldiers, once in a storm repeating her Antietam experience with hot gruel!

Vast sums of money, poured out by the generous American people, were placed at her disposal for relief to the suffering and destitute. A sufficient sum in ready cash she always kept on hand, in case a telegram came when the banks were closed; for there must be no delay in the Red Cross's starting on its mission of mercy.

The world over Clara Barton was known and loved and honored. The German emperor gave her the order of the iron cross, which at

Portrait of Clara Barton, 1904

that time had been awarded only for heroism on the battlefield. Queen Victoria herself pinned an English decoration on her dress. The Duke of Baden, Serbia, the Prince of Jerusalem all gave her honors; and her home was decorated with the flags of all the nations.

Dying at ninety, Clara Barton, retiring and bashful, had given fifty years of service to suffering humanity, working always on the firing line. David's born nurse became head nurse to all the nation. The angel of the battle-field, as the soldiers loved to call her, became the country's angel of mercy.

And in the Red Cross Society, building perhaps better than she knew, Clara Barton gave the opportunity for every American citizen, man or woman or little child, to share in her work of love and mercy.

Chapter 22

တ

Foes Become Friends

Even in the fiercest heat of the war for the Union, Americans did not forget that they were brothers. Veteran soldiers remember it now with more sincerity, because they fought more than a quarter of a century ago for a cause which they deemed the right. Many incidents of individual experiences of the war have been published of late years. The main point in all such incidents is the

Guerrilla Warfare, by Albert Bierstadt, 1862

eagerness with which the kindness of soldiers on the other side is extolled.

There is much in these incidents which may seem sentimental to the generation which was born after the war. But to Americans who remember how mighty were the interests involved in it, and how desperate was the struggle, these signs of the deep cordial peace which now exists between the North and South have a most pathetic and lofty meaning.

Only men who could nobly risk their fortunes and their love for a cause they held to be right could clasp hands when the struggle was over with forgiveness so true and complete.

Let us read of a few such incidents told by veteran soldiers of both sides at the annual reunions.

&

A private in a New Jersey regiment took part in a skirmish in which he was shot in the ankle, and again by a mini ball under the shoulder-blade, through the right lung. He was left for dead on the field. When he revived, he was surrounded by the Confederates. He lay for hours in an agony of pain and thirst, but summoned courage at last to ask a young lad for a drink.

The boy put his hand on his bayonet, saying, "I would never give you this," and passed on. Then suddenly turning, he said, "We are not as bad as you think us," and, stooping, gently lifted the head of the wounded man, and put a canteen to his lips.

A battery was placed near to where he lay, and one of the gunners, a man from Alabama, propped him up on his own blanket, brought a bucket of water and put it within reach, and came to him several times during the night to change his position. The next day a Southern doctor cut off his leg; he was carried to the hospital in Fredericksburg, and there was nursed by the good women of the town, one of whom he afterwards married.

&

At the reunion in Gettysburg, a few years ago, of the old soldiers from the North and South, who had fought against each other on that battle-field, many touching little incidents occurred that showed how cordial was the good-feeling now existing between the former enemies.

"Just here," said a crippled New-Yorker, stopping on the corner of a field, "my leg was shot off."

"And just here," said a man beside him, the sleeve of whose gray coat hung empty, "I lost my arm."

The two men became friends at once, pitched a tent on the spot that had been so eventful to both, and there "kept house" together during the whole time of the reunion. Each found the other to be a man of sense, high principle, and good-feeling. They will probably remain friends for life.

So many of the once bitter foes exchanged coats, canteens, and knapsacks, in token of good-will, that it became almost impossible to distinguish Northern from Southern soldiers. They pitched their tents together, most of the men preferring to camp again, instead of going to the hotels, in order that they might meet their old antagonists more freely, and discuss every incident of the battle, about the bivouac fires.

A Northern officer brought to Gettysburg a sword, gold-handled and set with jewels, which he had taken from a young Southerner. After the war was over he had tried in vain to restore it. He now gave it to the commandant of the corps to which its owner belonged, in the hope that it might reach him at last.

A large man and a very small one met on the street.

Prisoners from the Front, by Winslow Homer, 1866

"I think I have seen you before," said the small man.

"Yes, I took you prisoner," was the reply. Whereupon they shook hands heartily, took dinner together, and the next day brought a photographer to the spot where they had fought, and had their pictures taken standing with uncovered heads and clasped hands.

৪০

An old Pennsylvania farmer, after reading an account of this celebration at Gettysburg, in which both Union and Confederate soldiers bore a part, said, "I went to Gettysburg the night after the battle in 1863, and helped to bury the dead.

"One lad, I remember, in a gray uniform, whom we dragged from under a heap of dead bodies, was still breathing. He was but a pretty, chubby-faced schoolboy. We brought the surgeon, and worked with him for an hour, but it was too late, he was too far gone to feel the probe. He turned uneasily, smiling and muttering something, which showed that he thought he was back at home.

"'Mother! dear mother!' he said, and tried to lift his arms. Then came the fearful choking, and he was dead.

"Close beside him was the body of a private, belonging to the Sixty-eighth Pennsylvania. He was a young, firmly built man, with a face which, even in death, was gentle and kindly. His sunburned skin and horny hands showed him to have been a farmer.

"In his breast pocket we found a letter from 'Jenny,' with a few words about the crops and the poultry; but the letter was mainly 'Baby,' its doings and sayings, and at the bottom was a great blot made by Baby's own hand.

"Next his heart was a little photograph of a sweet-faced girl and a child, evidently Jenny and the baby.

"We buried the two men side by side.

"The blue and gray coated soldiers, the other day, were talking, and laughing, and fraternizing together over their graves, and near by, the corner-stone of a church, dedicated to the 'Prince of Peace,' was laid.

"But it seemed to me as if those two gallant boys who fought against one another here, each for a cause which he deemed just, must have long ago met elsewhere, and recognized each other as friends, and soldiers under one Captain."

&

The reception at Atlanta, in the fall of 1881, of the hero of the "March through Georgia," was a striking example of the generosity and warm-hearted forgetfulness of the Southern people. A Southern writer pleads for a better understanding with these people, with whom we were once at war, and draws the following vivid sketch of General Sherman's two visits to Atlanta: —

"He was at Atlanta once — and he looked the city over. I may say he felt it over. He made the acquaintance of its citizens, and its citizens made his acquaintance. The acquaintance may be said to have been mutual if not cordial. It was a decidedly warm acquaintance. When that stern commander got through with the city it looked with its bare and blackened chimneys like a forest of girdlings. Not a building of consequence was left.

"Seventeen years go by, and the man at whose order the city of Atlanta went up in smoke to

The Road March, by Julian Scott, 1879

come down in ashes, is invited by the authorities of the Exposition, a majority of whom were citizens of Atlanta, to return to that city as a guest.

"I said to myself, How will they receive him as they remember their beautiful homes, their business blocks, their churches reduced to ashes, their city which on one day stood fair and beautiful as a bride in the light, and which on the next was a heap of shapeless ruins?

"I secured my seat early and near the stand in the judges' hall, that I might study the problem of contending emotions, this phenomenon of a people rising superior to their prejudices and even to their very memories. For half an hour the people filed in till the hall was packed. I overheard the conversation which went on about me. One man from Louisville declared it was adding insult to injury — Sherman's return to Atlanta. Two others immediately took him to task. They said to him, 'Do not talk in that way. We live here. Sherman burned our property; but he did it in the heat of war. While war lasted we fought him; but the war is over, and General Sherman has come here to-day as the guest of Atlanta.'

"Presently the hero entered with his comrades of the Mexican War, many of them former generals of the Confederate army. Instantly there was an ovation of applause and waving of handkerchiefs. But I said, 'This may be intended for the Southern generals.' The speech was made and the exercises were about to close, when from all parts of the house there arose one universal and prolonged cry of 'Sherman! Sherman! Sherman!' And when he stepped from his place among his comrades and mounted the stand, the applause arose to a deafening roar.

"I said, 'This is one of the grandest displays of magnanimity to a former foe that the world has ever witnessed.'"

⌒
The Brave Men Who Fought for the Union

Nearly a generation has passed away since the breaking out of the war, and many of those now living know but little of the soldier's sacrifices. These should not be forgotten; the nation cannot afford to have them blotted out. They sacrificed for a time all the domestic relations of life. This may appear to some as a very small sacrifice to make. But ask that man who, on that eventful

The Departure of the Volunteer, by Felix Octavius Carr Darley, 1865

Union Refugees, by George W. Pettit, 1865

morning, kissed his wife good-by, and pressed his little child to his breast for the last time, as he shouldered his knapsack and marched away; or ask the smooth-faced lad who went forth to battle, with his mother's kiss damp upon his brow; and they will tell you of a fearful experience that raged within their hearts. This is one of the greatest sacrifices that men can be called upon to make for the country, and none but patriotic men can make it. They sacrificed the conveniences and comforts of home for the inconveniences and sufferings of the field. No army was ever marshalled upon the globe, that left such homes of comfort and luxury as did the Union army, in the war of the rebellion. They exchanged the mansion of comfort for the miserable shelter tent; the soft, clean bed, for a soldier's blanket spread upon the hard ground; good wholesome food, for the scanty rations of a soldier; lives of ease and healthy labor, for the exhaustion and weariness of forced marches; they threw aside for a period of years the personal liberty so dear to every American citizen, and took upon themselves a species of slavery, to be commanded by other men who were frequently their inferiors in all save military rank. They exchanged a life of comparative safety for one filled with a thousand dangers; they stepped forth from the peaceful circles of safety, within which so many remained, and boldly stood forth in the way where death passed by; and there bravely battled for the principles of liberty and justice. All these sacrifices were made for the salvation of the Republic.

These men suffered without complaint. What a lesson may be learned from their example! I wonder if the young people of our day ever stop to think how much their fathers and grandfathers who fought the battles of the Union suffered, sleeping on the hard, frozen ground, the cold winds sweeping over them, with nothing but their thin, ragged clothing to protect them from the elements, marching barefooted over the rough roads where their tracks were stained with blood that flowed from their lacerated feet, weary and exhausted, famishing with hunger when the government had no bread to give them; lying for days on the battle-fields between the contending lines, with broken limbs and mangled bodies, the sun pouring its deadly rays upon them, without food, their lips and throats parching with thirst, no medical aid, and their gaping wounds festering in the intense heat. All this they endured without murmuring, to preserve the Union. What an example they have set for us to follow! The patient sufferings of our soldiers through those four years of war should be held up as object lessons before our American youth, for all the years to come, that their hearts may be moulded in the same patriotic love and devotion for the country's welfare.

Our soldiers were brave men, and faced dangers fearlessly. The nation, I fear, is forgetting those deeds of bravery too rapidly. If we could only pass along those battle lines once more, and gather up those feats of individual daring, so many of which occurred in every regiment — deeds, which, if they had been performed in the Spartan wars, or in the days of the Crusaders, or of Napoleon the

The Return of the Volunteer, by Felix Octavius Carr Darley, 1865

First, would have been recorded on the pages of history, and would thrill the passing generations as they read! I wish we could gather up the unwritten history of the war — the deeds that were performed by heroes whose names were never known outside the ranks where they fought, or the beloved circle of friends at home, and which, if preserved, would fill volumes. These soldiers were as modest as they were brave, and many of them have never spoken of the wild adventures through which they passed, or of the narrow escapes, the hand-to-hand encounters which they experienced, or of the shot and shells that went tearing past them, so near that the slightest deviation from their onward course would have caused their death. These events are locked up within their own breasts, cherished as sacred reminders of God's providence in preserving their lives. But some evening, as you sit beside some maimed hero, draw him forth from his seclusion, get him to unfold that secret chapter of his life, and as he proceeds with that wonderful narrative, you will decide that I have not exaggerated when I have claimed that the soldiers who fought for the Union were brave men.

The Lost Cause, attributed to Henry Mosler, 1869

References

Chapter 1:

Tappan, Eva March. 1906. *American hero stories* (pp. 237-245). Boston, New York [etc.]; Houghton, Mifflin and Company.

Groetzinger, Thomas. 1919. *Heroes of national history* (pp. 150-158). Philadelphia; Franklin publishing and supply company.

Chapter 2:

Daffan, Katie. 1912. *Texas heroes; a reader for schools* (pp. 104-113). Boston, New York [etc.]; B. H. Sanborn & co.

Chapter 3:

Miller, Francis Trevelyan. circa 1909. *Hero tales from American life* (pp. 365-368). New York; The Christian herald.

Chapter 4:

Daffan, Katie. 1912. *Texas heroes; a reader for schools* (pp. 114-135). Boston, New York [etc.]; B. H. Sanborn & co.

Chapter 5:

Holland, Rupert Sargent. 1913. *Historic adventures; tales from American history* (pp. 165-180). Philadelphia; G.W. Jacobs & Company.

Chapter 6:

Eggleston, Edward. circa 1895. *Stories of American life and adventure* (pp. 171-177). New York; American Book Company.

Chapter 7:

Blaisdell, Albert Franklin. 1890. *Stories of the Civil War* (pp. 8-10). Boston; Lee and Shepard.

Chapter 8:

Uhrbrock, Richard Stephen; Owens, Albert Alexander. circa 1922. *Famous Americans* (pp. 318-326). Indianapolis; The Bobbs-Merrill Company.

Chapter 9:

Groetzinger, Thomas. 1919. *Heroes of national history* (pp. 243-247). Philadelphia; Franklin publishing and supply company.

Chapter 10:

Stimpson, Mary Stoyell. 1915. *The child's book of American biography* (pp. 62-74). Boston; Little, Brown and company.

Chapter 11:

Brooks, Eldridge Streeter. 1897. *The True Story of U.S. Grant, the American Soldier* (pp.206-219). Boston; Lothrop Publishing Co.

Chapter 12:

Coe, Fanny E. 1914. *Makers of the nation* (pp. 342-345). New York; American Book Company.

Chapter 13:

The Companion Library. 1905. *Heroes of History* (pp. 26-33). Perry Mason Co.

Chapter 14:

Blaisdell, Albert Franklin. 1890. *Stories of the Civil War* (pp. 36-41). Boston; Lee and Shepard.

Chapter 15:

Baldwin, James. 1907. *An American book of golden deeds* (pp. 167-169). New York; American Book Company.
Humphrey, Grace. 1919. *Women in American History* (pp. 154-163). The Bobbs-Merrill Company.

Chapter 16:

Blaisdell, Albert Franklin. 1890. *Stories of the Civil War* (pp. 54-61). Boston; Lee and Shepard.

Chapter 17:

Humphrey, Grace. 1919. *Women in American History* (pp. 179-188). The Bobbs-Merrill Company.

Chapter 18:

Blaisdell, Albert F. 1890. *Stories of the Civil War* (pp. 187-192). Boston; Lee and Shepard.

References

Chapter 19:

Horton, Edith. 1914. *A group of famous women; stories of their lives* (pp. 61-72). Boston, New York; D. C. Heath and company.

Chapter 20:

Baldwin, James. 1907. *An American book of golden deeds* (pp. 248-255). New York; American Book Company.

Chapter 21:

Humphrey, Grace. 1919. *Women in American History* (pp. 189-206) The Bobbs-Merrill Company.

Chapter 22:

Blaisdell, Albert Franklin. 1890. *Stories of the Civil War* (pp. 222-229). Boston; Lee and Shepard.

Chapter 23:

Blaisdell, Albert Franklin. 1890. *Stories of the Civil War* (pp. 233-236). Boston; Lee and Shepard.